PEN[illegible]

Charlene Lunnon and Lisa Hoodless both live in Hastings, East [illegible] Charlene with her partner, William, and baby daughter, Rubie-rae; Lisa with her son, Kyle.

Abducted

CHARLENE LUNNON

and LISA HOODLESS

with Gill Paul

PENGUIN BOOKS

PENGUIN BOOKS

Published by the Penguin Group
Penguin Books Ltd, 80 Strand, London WC2R 0RL, England
Penguin Group (USA) Inc., 375 Hudson Street, New York, New York 10014, USA
Penguin Group (Canada), 90 Eglinton Avenue East, Suite 700, Toronto, Ontario, Canada M4P 2Y3
(a division of Pearson Penguin Canada Inc.)
Penguin Ireland, 25 St Stephen's Green, Dublin 2, Ireland (a division of Penguin Books Ltd)
Penguin Group (Australia), 250 Camberwell Road, Camberwell, Victoria 3124, Australia
(a division of Pearson Australia Group Pty Ltd)
Penguin Books India Pvt Ltd, 11 Community Centre, Panchsheel Park, New Delhi – 110 017, India
Penguin Group (NZ), 67 Apollo Drive, Rosedale, North Shore 0632, New Zealand
(a division of Pearson New Zealand Ltd)
Penguin Books (South Africa) (Pty) Ltd, 24 Sturdee Avenue, Rosebank,
Johannesburg 2196, South Africa

Penguin Books Ltd, Registered Offices: 80 Strand, London WC2R 0RL, England

www.penguin.com

First published 2009
001

Typeset by Rowland Phototypesetting Ltd, Bury St Edmunds, Suffolk
Printed in England by Clays Ltd, St Ives plc

ISBN 978-1-405-91002-6

www.greenpenguin.co.uk

MIX
Paper from responsible sources
FSC www.fsc.org FSC™ C018179

Penguin Books is committed to a sustainable future for our business, our readers and our planet. This book is made from Forest Stewardship Council™ certified paper.

ALWAYS LEARNING PEARSON

Foreword

On 28th June 1995 a man was released from prison in Kent, where he had served four years for the kidnapping of an eleven-year-old girl and the attempted kidnapping of a seventeen-year-old. A month later he moved to Eastbourne. This was in the days before the Sex Offenders' Register and he slipped quietly off the police radar.

In 1998, 14 miles along the coast in Hastings, two young girls were becoming firm friends. They liked clothes and sweets and computer games and the Spice Girls. After they had reached their tenth birthdays, their parents decided they were responsible enough to walk to school together every morning without adult supervision. After all, it was only a ten-minute walk.

The man didn't have any friends, or a job. He lived alone in a dreary flat above a shopping centre. His only interest in life was pretty young girls . . .

PART I

1

Charlene

Lisa and I were best friends from the day I started at Christ Church Primary School in June 1998, when I was nine years old. I'd moved schools quite a few times by then because I'd been in and out of foster care since I was very small, but at last I had a proper home with my dad and I hoped that I could finally settle somewhere and make some real friends.

Christ Church Primary seemed much bigger than any school I'd been to before, with a confusing layout. There were two different staircases up the middle – the little kids went one way while the bigger kids went the other and I thought I would never be able to find my way around. A boy called Dan was assigned to guide me for the day, pointing out where the toilets were and so forth, but although he seemed nice I felt nervous and too scared to strike up a conversation with anyone.

In the Year 4 classroom, I'd only just started writing the sentences the teacher asked us to copy out when the lead snapped off the end of my pencil. I looked in my pencil case and realised I'd forgotten to bring a sharpener.

'Does anyone have a sharpener I can borrow?' I whispered timidly to the group sitting nearest.

A voice behind me said, 'I've got a Spice Girls sharpener.' I turned round to see a girl with short, curly, light brown hair and two round bunches on the sides, like Princess Leia in *Star Wars*.

'Thanks,' I said. I loved the Spice Girls. Baby Spice had been my first favourite but now I preferred Posh because she was so sophisticated and I liked the way she dressed.

'You can keep it,' the girl said, and I smiled shyly at her.

'You're new,' she said. 'What school did you go to before?'

'I've just moved down to Hastings to stay with my dad. I was in London before.'

'Where do you live?'

I told her the name of our road.

'I live just one road down from yours,' she said. 'My name's Lisa. I'll play with you at break time if you like, if you haven't got anyone else to play with.'

I nodded and grinned and was about to say 'Yes, please,' when the teacher told us to stop talking and get on with our work.

At break time we walked out to the playground together, chatting all the way. I really liked her shoes, which were a bright blue, green and yellow mix with foam rubber soles and a strap across the top. She liked the hairband I was wearing with my name spelt out across it in different-coloured letters on a black velvet background. I liked her funky nail varnish – blue with yellow dots – and the fact that she was so little and sweet and happy. She smiled the whole time, as if she didn't have a single care in the world.

I invited her up to my dad's house that evening and she arrived wearing a little pink cardigan and denim hot-pants and those blue sandals and we just hit it off. We quickly found out that we both collected teddy bears and arranged to swap some with each other. We liked playing Crash Bandicoot on PlayStation, and doing our hair and playing card games like Crazy Ace. The time just flew when we were together, and we never ran out of things to chat about. Dad was happy that I'd found a friend, and so was I.

It was only two weeks till the end of term, but then it was the summer holidays and we spent the whole summer playing together, either at my house or at Lisa's. She had swings in her garden, but her dad was very strict so we spent more time up at mine, having water fights in the paddling pool, making little camps, walking to the Spar to get ice creams or sneaking up to throw water balloons at her older brother James. She often stayed overnight at mine, although I never stayed at hers because her dad didn't like noise. I'd never been allowed to have a friend staying over before, but I loved it. We would stay awake for hours, whispering secrets to each other and telling each other about our lives.

I had quite a story to tell, I suppose, and it was very different to Lisa's background. She had a brother and two sisters, and parents who were married and lived together – just a nice, normal family, or so it seemed to me. There was nothing normal about my childhood, though it was a bit more settled now that I was at last living with my dad, his wife Philomena and her daughter Ceri-Jane. It had taken a long journey to get there.

My mum was an alcoholic and a heroin addict and she kept trying to go clean but couldn't manage, even when she was pregnant with me. I was born prematurely and addicted to methadone, which meant I was very small and couldn't breathe for myself, so I had to be kept in an incubator in hospital for several months before I was allowed home.

I had two half-sisters, Carol and Rose, but they were much older than me – twenty years or so – and had their own homes. Carol had kids of her own, and I saw her from time to time but I hardly saw Rose at all. I also had a couple of much older half-brothers but I'd never met them and didn't know anything about them.

Mum and I lived in a West London maisonette that was filthy and always full of different men who were coming and going, injecting drugs then disappearing into the bedroom with her. I'd be left on my own watching horror movies on the telly while they groaned and panted in the next room. I knew exactly what they were doing. One time when I was three I walked in while she was having sex with someone and I asked, 'Mummy, where's the cookie jar?'

'It's in the cupboard,' she told me, stopping briefly.

So I went downstairs and got a biscuit. It didn't faze me at all. I don't know when I learned the facts of life but it felt as though I'd always known.

Once I was asleep on Mum's lap and I woke up to find

a man trying to put his penis into her mouth. That's what her so-called 'friends' were like.

Some of the men shouted at me and pushed me around a bit but none of them ever harmed me. They quite often fought with each other, though. I remember one fight when a guy got stabbed in the bum and there was blood all over our sofa. I didn't like to sit on it after that because every time I looked at it I felt sick.

There was never any food in the cupboards so I was often starving, but if Mum took me to nursery school they'd give me school lunches of pizza or sandwiches or roast chicken. We didn't have dinner times at home. I'd get fed when Mum could be bothered, if she had anything in the house. I have an early memory of sitting in front of the television eating mushy peas out of a tin and thinking they were delicious.

I loved my mum to pieces, though. When she was being nice, she was great fun and used to give me lovely cuddles. But that could change in a heartbeat. I didn't know what drugs she was taking but I knew whenever she'd taken some because from being my smiling, affectionate mother she would suddenly change and would be off her face, just lying on the sofa, eyes rolling back, not doing anything. It was worse when she was drunk because she got violent then; either that or we'd go out and I'd have to sit outside the pub waiting for her for hours on end.

Once, I picked her some flowers from the garden but when I came into the flat to give them to her, she was drunk.

'I've got you some flowers,' I said, holding them out and beaming from ear to ear, sure that she would be pleased with me.

'Get out of the way,' she snarled and pushed me over, before she staggered upstairs with some man and locked the bedroom door behind her. I still remember how shocked and hurt I felt sitting on the hall floor, clutching my straggly flowers and staring after her.

Sometimes I asked about my dad, but Mum hated him with a passion and wouldn't tell me anything except that he was a thieving, lying, no-good junkie who was probably in jail; so I stopped asking after a while.

When I was four, social services stepped in. Seemingly I was suffering from malnutrition, with my ribs sticking out, and they decided enough was enough. I was taken into care and assigned to foster parents. Between the ages of four and six, I think I had about four different sets of foster parents. There were definitely benefits to this – I got fed, my hair was brushed, I got a story read to me at bedtime, I had nice clean clothes – but all the time I missed Mum. I would much rather have been back with her than living with strangers in their house. None of them were as much fun as she could be when she was sober.

Once a week, we had supervised visits when Mum came to see me in a special hall with lots of toys on the floor. I looked forward to her visits like mad, but she didn't always turn up and if she did, she might be off her face. She kept applying to have me back and when I was five I did go home to live with her again for a few months. She was clean of drugs but still drinking. Some days she would be the most brilliant mum in the world to me, then the next she was so ratty you didn't want to be anywhere near her. I suppose social services still didn't think she was taking proper care of me because before long I was whipped off into foster care again.

Meanwhile, I had started at primary school but it was hard to make friends because I felt so different from all of them. They had proper mums and dads and nice houses, and they had birthday parties and Christmas stockings and went for sleepovers at each other's houses. Obviously I couldn't have anyone to stay over at Mum's, and when I was in care, it was a complicated process with forms to be filled in before I could have anyone back to play, so I never bothered. I changed schools a few times as I changed foster parents, so any friends I made were left behind anyway.

Then, when I was six, my dad's sister Vera and her husband Harry said that they would foster me. They had two boys, Scott and Steven, who were much older than me. Scott was about seventeen when I arrived and Steven had already left home. My Auntie Vera was absolutely lovely. I think maybe she had always wanted a girl because she started buying me lots of girly presents, like pink Barbie shoes, and fifty-two Polly Pockets along with the Polly Pocket village, and not only did I have lots of Barbies but I also had the camper van, the horse, the house and everything to go with it. My whole bedroom was Barbie pink, from the bedcovers to the wastepaper basket to the lampshade.

Auntie Vera took me to drama classes and singing lessons and Irish dance club and I loved anything to do with performing. I didn't like school so much though. I was diagnosed as dyslexic and no matter how much they give you the soft soap, I always felt self-conscious that I couldn't read very well. I was way behind the rest of the class and that made me feel as though I must be stupid.

Once I was living at Auntie Vera's, my dad came back into my life. He came round one Sunday soon after I arrived and we all sat in the sitting room together having tea and cakes. I was worried because Mum had always told me he was evil and no good, so I hung back a bit and didn't go over to give him a hug or anything.

'Do you remember me?' he asked first and I shook my head, then I worried that might seem rude.

'We've met a couple of times before,' he said, 'When you were living at your mum's, but you were very young at the time.'

He had a nice face and he looked straight at me when he was talking to me, which I liked. He explained to me that he had been a heroin addict, like Mum, but had signed himself into a rehab centre in Bexhill and got clean. He told me that as soon as he heard I'd been taken into care, he'd gone to the courts to try to get custody of me or even just to be allowed to visit me but his requests were always denied because of his past record, which included some time in jail for theft back when he was a drug addict.

'I'm living down in Hastings now,' he said, 'Working as

a counsellor at a rehabilitation centre. That means I help other people to come off drugs.'

'Could you help my mum?' I asked innocently, and there was a hush in the room as the adults all looked at each other.

'I don't know if she's ready to stop yet,' he replied at last. 'But if you like, you could come down and visit me in Hastings some time and I'll show you around. It's just by the seaside. Would you like that?'

I felt a bit odd because I didn't really know him, even if he was my dad. 'Could Auntie Vera come too?' I asked.

'Yes, of course. And your Uncle Harry.'

We didn't go down straight away but I found myself beginning to look forward to Dad's visits. I liked the way he talked to me, like an equal instead of a grown-up talking to a child, and he always listened to what I told him and remembered to ask me questions the next time. If I said I had a maths test at school, he would remember to ask how it went. He remembered that I had a friend called Toni and he'd always ask 'How's Toni?' when he came. After a while he started taking me out for lunch and he always let me go to McDonald's. I loved McDonald's. It was my absolute favourite place.

I still saw Mum on supervised visits at weekends, and I started playing up a bit and blackmailing her.

'If you don't buy me a chocolate bar,' I said, 'I'll go and live with my dad.'

She hated that thought so she always bought me the chocolate bar. 'You can't do that, sweetie,' she coaxed.

'You and me are going to live together again, just as soon as I knock some sense into the authorities.'

By the time I was eight, things were much better. Mum had stopped taking drugs and hadn't even been drinking for six months because she was determined that I should be allowed to come back and live with her. Social services had said she just had to manage a couple more weeks of staying clean and then I could go home, so I was really excited. Every Saturday, she came to the children's centre for a supervised visit, and she always brought me a Lion bar, which was my favourite chocolate bar. She looked really well, she'd got a nice new flat and she'd got engaged to a lovely bloke called Malcolm, who wasn't in the drugs scene. She promised me that she had left all her old druggie friends behind and she only saw nice people now. I couldn't wait to go home because she was my mum and I loved her to pieces.

Then one Saturday, Mum didn't turn up. Uncle Harry took me to the centre for a visit and we sat together in the big hall with all the toys in the middle and the other children who were having supervised visits all messing around, and we waited and waited for over an hour. As we sat there in silence, I felt a cold fear crawling over my skin. I knew something bad had happened. She wouldn't have forgotten. She wanted me back with her so much that the only reason she wouldn't have come that day would be if she was dead. I actually thought that. It was as if somehow I knew.

It was two days later before it was confirmed. I was watching telly with Auntie Vera and Uncle Harry when the doorbell rang. I went to answer it and it was my half-sister Carol.

'I've got bad news,' she said bluntly. 'Mum's dead.'

My worst fears had come true. I just stood there and couldn't react. I didn't ask how; I knew it had to be drug-related.

Carol stood fidgeting on the doorstep for a bit, then she said, 'I'll let you know when the funeral is,' and off she went.

'Who is it?' my aunt's voice called from the sitting room.

'It was Carol,' I told her going back into the room. 'She says my mum is dead.'

Auntie Vera gave a little scream and jumped up to hug me, but I didn't cry or anything. I felt completely numb. Shortly afterwards I went out to play with my friends outside and I didn't say anything about it to them. It was as if it hadn't happened.

A week later I went to Mum's funeral, in a little room at a crematorium, and still I didn't get upset. There were only a few people there because most of Mum's friends had died from drug overdoses before her, and it was over very quickly.

After the funeral, I kept having dreams in which I woke up and Mum was still alive. I don't think the reality had sunk in. It was about a year later when I suddenly had a delayed reaction to it all. It's as if I'd been given an anaesthetic and after a year it wore off and the grief burst out in a great big emotional rush. It was then that I asked Auntie Vera what had happened and she explained it to me.

It seems that Mum had had a massive argument with Malcolm and he stormed off for the evening, leaving her at home on her own. She was so upset that she fell off the wagon and took some heroin. Because she'd been clean for six months, her body had lost its ability to cope with the drug and all her organs just shut down. Malcolm came back and found her in bed, where she seemed as though she was sleeping, so he just climbed in beside her. It was only when he rolled over to give her a hug at six in the morning that he realised she was stone cold.

I cried all the time for months after that. I started having problems at school because I couldn't concentrate on lessons, and I kept asking Auntie Vera if I could take days off because I was so upset. She was lovely to me right through that period but it was my mum I wanted and I couldn't have her. I couldn't ever hug her or laugh and joke with her again. It was the hardest thing I'd ever had to cope with. It hurt so much.

Even now, when Lisa and I were whispering secrets to each other after we'd snuggled down in our duvets, I couldn't tell her about everything that had happened to me. Some things were so bad and so painful that I couldn't tell anyone, ever. Losing Mum was just the beginning.

2

Lisa

When Charlene told me about everything that had happened to her in her life, I could only imagine what that must be like. Our family seemed very dull and ordinary by comparison, but secretly I was glad. I thought that Charlene must have had some terrible experiences and I hoped I'd never have to go through anything as bad. I was happy feeling safe and secure at home.

We lived in a maisonette in Hastings, upstairs from my granddad, my mum's dad, whom I was very close to. He lived in the flat below, and I'd be in and out of his place all day long. He used to be a teacher before he retired, so he helped me with my homework after school – but he'd never give me the answers, and instead made me work them out for myself. He'd give me juice and biscuits while we worked, and find bits of paper for me to do my drawings on when we finished. He loved my art – I was especially good at copying cartoon characters – and was always encouraging me to draw pictures for him.

Upstairs, there were four of us children – my brother James, who is two years older than me, my sister Christine, who is two years younger, and the baby,

Georgie, who is nine years younger than me. My dad was very strict. We all had to sit around the dinner table together every evening and we weren't allowed to leave until we had cleaned our plates and everyone else was finished as well. Dad hated noise and the kind of mess and racket that children make, so we weren't allowed in the front room when he was watching telly in case we disturbed him. We were rarely allowed to have friends over to play, and Dad never let us have anyone over to stay the night, even though we begged. He said he worked very hard and needed his rest when he was at home. He worked as a gardener for the council, doing the flowers along the seafront, and he just loved gardening. He was very good at it, I think.

My mum didn't work. I used to think she was very beautiful, with long black hair and a slim figure, but she could be a bit dopey and I couldn't really confide in her if I had a problem because she never kept secrets. She was always going out with her friends while Dad stayed at home to babysit for us, and if she were at home, she'd have friends round to sit and gossip with her over a coffee or a glass of wine.

I was a very girly girl, with my Barbies and my pink bike. Dad built us a Wendy house in the back garden that had carpets and curtains and some old car seats to sit on and I liked taking my friends in there to play cards when Dad let them come over. In my bedroom, I had posters of the Spice Girls, Leonardo di Caprio and Snow White, from the Disney film. I shared my room with my sister Christine and I kept my half of that bedroom spotlessly clean and tidy – in fact, people used to compare me to Monica from *Friends*, who is obsessive about cleaning. I could tell instantly if anyone had been in, because everything had its own place and I'd notice if things were moved by even a millimetre or two. I'd know if Christine had borrowed my shoes because she never put them back in exactly the right place, and I knew when my brother or sister had found the latest hiding place for my money pot and helped themselves to fifty pence. It used to make me furious but no matter how hard I tried to think of good new hiding places, they always seemed to find them.

I liked primary school and did well at most subjects – except for science, which I hated. I won a competition once for a story I wrote about a rainbow fish, and I was good at art, reading and maths. I had plenty of friends – Samantha, who had been a close friend since nursery school; Lisa, the chatterbox with the same name as me; and Luke, who was sometimes mean to me because he was a boy and boys that age aren't meant to be nice to girls, but who was basically a friend as well. And when I was ten, I had a boyfriend called Stevie. He had black hair and pale skin, and we used to go out on our bikes together or I'd go round to his house to play on his computer. I was his girlfriend for about a year, but we only kissed once, and that was just a little peck.

As soon as Charlene arrived at Christ Church Primary and I lent her my Spice Girls sharpener, we were best friends. She had long dark brown hair that was held back in a pretty hairband and seemed quite quiet – although I soon found out that was just because she was new to the school and feeling a bit shy. Once the holidays started, we spent hours and hours at her house. Her dad, Keith, made me feel completely welcome and said I could stay over at weekends whenever I wanted to. He was obviously very pleased to have Charlene living with him, and wanted to see her happy, so if she asked me to come and stay, then I could.

Even though her dad doted on her, Charlene didn't have a totally easy life at home. I felt sorry for her, because I could see that she didn't get on very well with her stepsister Ceri-Jane, who was always accusing her of messing with her make-up and touching her things. When they passed in the hall, Ceri-Jane would say things like 'Hello, smelly!' Charlene would ignore her and pretend not to care, but I could see that it hurt her feelings. Her stepmother, Philomena, didn't seem too keen on Charlene being around the place either – she was always snapping at her and telling her that her dad was spoiling her. She didn't seem to like me much either – I don't think she liked any of Charlene's friends. We never asked her for anything because we knew she would say 'no' but Keith was so kind, he would give us whatever we wanted, so we were always asking him for sweets or this and that. I loved it round at Charlene's house because it felt so relaxed compared to my home, if we ignored Ceri-Jane and Philomena, and we were really allowed to do whatever we liked.

When we were playing, Charlene was usually the one who would be in charge. I've never been a bossy kind of person and I was quite happy to just go along with her.

She usually chose the games we played and decided the rules. When we realised we both had lots of teddy bears, we decided to swap some and I don't know how but I ended up giving her three of my bears for the one of hers that I wanted, but I didn't mind.

I was an innocent nine-year-old, and my childhood had been very sheltered. Char was much more streetwise than me and I listened open-mouthed when she told me bits and pieces about her background: that her mother had been a drug addict and that she'd been taken into care when she was four because she wasn't being looked after properly. She had only come to live with her dad that year even though he'd been applying through the courts to have her for ages. I thought it was a very sad story and I felt so sorry for her when she told me that her mother had died. I couldn't imagine anything worse than losing your mum. After Charlene confided in me about such an awful thing, I felt very close to her.

Charlene was more grown-up than me in other ways as well. We had a sex education class at school one day, where they told us about starting periods and growing breasts, and I thought periods sounded disgusting. When we came out of the lesson, I said to Charlene, 'Yuck! Imagine all that blood in your knickers.'

And she said, 'It's not that bad. Don't worry about it. I started mine earlier this year.'

I was amazed. 'But you're only nine. The teacher said in the lesson it might happen when you were eleven or twelve.'

She shrugged. 'I'm just an early developer.' Then she

said something I didn't understand at all. 'It means I could get pregnant now.'

I looked at her questioningly but she changed the subject. I had absolutely no idea how you got pregnant. I suppose I thought it was something that only happened when you got married. I knew babies grew in their mother's tummies because my mum had only just given birth to Georgie that year, but as to how they got there I hadn't a clue and I'd never thought to question it.

Because Charlene seemed more mature than me, and she was a good few inches taller, I suppose we slipped into a pattern where she looked after me, like a big sister. She would stand up to my brother if he was bullying me and cook meals for me at her place, and comfort me if I was upset. My brother James, who is two years older than me, used to beat me up sometimes and once he made me ride my bike all the way to Filsham School with him, which is about half an hour away, then he left me to find my way home on my own. I think he felt left out in our family, because there were three of us girls and no other boys, and maybe that's why he took it out on us sometimes – or maybe it's just an oldest child thing. Maybe all big brothers are the same.

In September, we went back to school. Now we were in Year Five, and very excited to be moving up and getting our new timetables. We were both kitted out in our new shoes and schoolbags. Now that we were ten years old, our parents decided that we were big enough to walk to school together: it was only ten minutes away and there were no main roads to cross. Charlene's stepmum

Philomena would walk her down to our house, then we'd set off on our own, chattering away about all sorts.

That's what we were doing on the morning of Tuesday 19 January 1999. Just going on our way to school, like any other day. Two small girls walking along the road, talking away to each other and expecting to be at school in just a few minutes.

3
Tuesday morning

Charlene

I was happy that year. I'd been living with Dad for eight months, and had settled down well. Philomena was very sweet to me at first, even though she grumbled all the time about Dad spoiling me. Then I think she began to resent the fact that she didn't get as much time on her own with him. Instead of him taking her out to do adult things when he had time off, they had to choose days out that I would enjoy, such as theme parks or fairgrounds. Sometimes I heard them arguing, and Phil would tell Dad that he was spoiling me, and I'd hear him say to her, 'Have a heart! Think of what the kid's been through, for Christ's sake!'

Ceri-Jane was so much older than me that we didn't become close, and I annoyed her by sometimes sneaking into her room and trying on her clothes and make-up – I was fascinated by all her big-girl things and wanted to try them out myself, even though I knew I shouldn't.

It was always going to be difficult, Dad's real daughter moving in with his new wife and teenage stepdaughter, but on the whole it wasn't too bad. I was happy because I had my dad, and I had my new best friend, Lisa. If I wanted anything, I only had to ask Dad and he'd get it for me. Phil hadn't wanted me to get a hamster because she said they were smelly but I insisted I would look after it all by myself and keep its cage clean, so Dad let me have one. It was a beautiful white and beige long-haired hamster, which I called Fluffy, and I took care of her, just like I'd promised.

I was enjoying school as well. We had a new teacher that year, a Canadian man called Mr Okrainetz. He was on an exchange scheme, and seemed much more enthusiastic and caring than our usual teachers. I liked him a lot. My favourite thing at school was when we were read stories, and he was especially good at that, putting on all the voices and making it sound more interesting with his funny accent.

On that Tuesday morning, it was quite cold and gloomy so I was wearing a black quilted coat over my school uniform. Actually, it was black on one side and blue on the other and you could wear it either way. I'd just got it for Christmas and was very pleased with it. Philomena was busy and couldn't walk me to Lisa's that day and I was running a bit late, so I phoned Lisa and asked her to walk up to meet me at the end of our close. When I hurried out, I could see her standing there in her orange quilted jacket and her little black school skirt, clutching her pink Spice Girls schoolbag.

'Hiya!' I called. 'Sorry I'm late.'

'Doesn't matter,' she said, linking her arm through mine. A car went by us, and Lisa frowned. 'I think that car's following me. I'm sure I saw it before, outside our house.'

'Yeah, right,' I said, rolling my eyes. Why on earth would anyone want to follow Lisa? 'Why don't we take the short cut past the garage and we can get some sweets?' I suggested. It wasn't much of a short cut; the distance was probably much the same, but once we'd got onto Cornfield Terrace, just past the garage, we only had to walk all the way down it and we'd be at the school.

'OK,' she agreed.

I bought some Haribos, which I loved, and Lisa bought a Creme Egg and we were both munching them as we turned into Cornfield Terrace. The pavement there is quite narrow, and on the left side there are the backs of all the houses from the street one further down, with gates leading into the back gardens. On the right are the front gardens and front doors of the houses in that road. We walked past the church and the pub at the top of the road, then we had to walk in single file to fit onto the narrow pavement. Lisa was in front.

We'd gone about ten steps down the road when we came upon some black bin bags that had been ripped open, probably by seagulls. Smelly rubbish was scattered all over the ground: used teabags, bashed-up tin cans, cardboard boxes, scrunched tissues, mushy food left-overs that looked like sick. We tiptoed around it, holding our noses and giggling. Lisa turned to say something to me and I noticed she was about to stand on a squashed potato that had gone all green and mouldy so I shoved her out of the way and she stumbled onto the road just as a car came along. A turquoise car. The driver braked and swerved slightly to avoid hitting her, and I thought he looked a bit annoyed with us, although he didn't beep the horn or anything.

'Sorry!' I said to Lisa. 'But look at that yucky potato you nearly stood in.'

'Eww, disgusting!' she exclaimed and we both started laughing as if it was really funny.

'What's worse?' I giggled. 'Getting run over by a car or stepping on a mushy green potato?'

Further down the road, the turquoise car stopped and the driver got out. It crossed my mind that he might be coming back to tell us off but instead he walked around and opened his boot, peering inside it as if he was looking for something. He was very tall and seemed quite old. That must be his house, I decided. He lives there and he's just getting something out of his boot to take inside.

Lisa and I were still giggling a bit as we reached him, but we stopped as he turned and came towards us.

'Sorry about that, girls,' he said, as he approached. 'I'm really glad I didn't hit you,' he said to Lisa. 'It wasn't your fault, don't worry about running into the road.'

'It's fine,' she said.

'Are you sure you're OK?'

She nodded, then asked, 'Do you have the time?'

He looked at his watch. 'Twenty-five to nine.'

Something about him made me feel uneasy. 'Come on, Lisa. We're late,' I said. 'We've got to hurry up.' We were supposed to be at school for quarter to nine and there was still quite a way to go.

I was starting to walk off when the driver put his arms around our shoulders. I didn't like his arm on me but it seemed rude to push it off. I gave a weird little laugh and Lisa said 'Yeah, OK,' and then I felt his grip tightening.

'Get in the car and do as I say,' he hissed, his fingers digging into my collar.

Lisa started screaming and he clapped his hand over her mouth, still holding onto my shoulder. I just stood there, frozen. I didn't do anything. I looked at Lisa and her face was going bright red from the effort of trying to scream with his big hand over her mouth, and she was struggling and kicking to get away. I didn't kick or scream. I just stood there in complete shock.

He picked Lisa up easily because she was so little, and he threw her into the boot of the car. I could have run away at that point because he was only holding onto my coat, but I was stunned, like a rabbit in headlights. I couldn't react. The only thought in my head was that I mustn't abandon Lisa and leave her on her own with him. I had to stay with her and try to protect her.

I looked up and down the road. There were houses all the way along. Why hadn't anyone come running out when Lisa screamed? Where were they all? Surely someone must be around at that time in the morning?

She was lying, stunned, on a tartan rug on the floor of his boot, staring up at me with big, terrified eyes.

'Get in!' the man urged, tugging at me, and I automatically lifted my leg and stepped into the boot. I just did it to stick with Lisa. I couldn't leave her on her own like that.

'What are you going to do with us?' I asked.

And he said, 'I want you for money. Do as you're told,'

then he pushed me down and slammed the lid of the boot.

It was pitch black inside and we were crushed up against each other, side by side, with our faces touching. She was crying really hard, asking me over and over what was happening to us, her whole body shaking, and I could feel the wetness of her tears and snot on my cheek. I was still in shock, my heart beating hard and my head buzzing. We felt him getting into the car and heard the door shutting then the engine started and we were moving. Where on earth would he take us?

I lay still, frozen with shock for quite a while longer. I get asthma attacks sometimes but I'd left my inhaler at school the day before. What would I do if I had an attack in that boot?

Finally I spoke. 'I know what he's going to do,' I said.

Lisa struggled to control her sobs and stammered, 'Wh-what?'

'He's going to rape us and murder us,' I said, and she gave a little scream and started crying even harder than before. I hadn't meant to upset her. I just knew for sure that's what it was all about. That's what was going to happen.

Lisa

I'd seen a turquoise car in my road that morning. It had been driving past when I came out of my house and I noticed the colour because it was quite bright and not a normal car colour. When I went up to meet Charlene I saw the same car again, this time going the way I was walking. But when I told her that I thought the car was following me and she dismissed it, I forgot about it. Charlene was right: that kind of thing only happened in films, not in our world. It was early morning and broad daylight and no one would ever dream anything bad could happen, especially in a tiny seaside resort like Hastings.

We walked up Church Road to the garage and turned down Cornfield Terrace and the car was still behind us, but I didn't click that that was unusual. Now I realise that he must have been driving really slowly, waiting round the corner, watching us the whole time. It must have suited him right down to the ground when we turned into Cornfield Terrace, which is a quiet one-way street. He saw his opportunity and knew it was then, or never.

When Charlene pushed me into the road to avoid the potato and the turquoise car had to swerve to avoid me, I watched it continue down the road and I thought, Thank God that car's gone. But then he pulled into a parking space up ahead and got out to open the boot, so I assumed he lived there. Char and I were still chattering and laughing about the potato and how disgusting it was so we didn't say anything to each other about him.

As we got closer, he came over to us and apologised for nearly hitting me. My parents had always taught me to be polite, so I said that was OK. Then I asked him the time, just as a way to end the conversation, so we could say 'We'd better go now.'

When he first put his arms around us, we gave each other an odd little grin, thinking it was some embarrassing grown-up joke and he was messing around with us. Then he suddenly said those terrifying words 'Get in the car and do as I say,' and everything changed. I started screaming and immediately he put his hand over my mouth. It was heavy and horrible, and shut off my screams and my breath. An instant later, he'd lifted me up without any trouble – I only weighed about four stone and he was a big, tall man so it was pretty easy for him – and went to throw me into the open boot of his car. I struggled hard, trying to kick my feet off the back of the car, but it did no good at all. He tossed me into the boot as if I was a bag of feathers. The shock made me stop screaming.

I stared out of the boot in utter panic. Charlene was standing there, looking back at me; she wasn't doing anything and I couldn't understand why. She seemed to be frozen to the spot, her eyes wide and staring. He yanked her coat and ordered her to get in, so she just got in beside me without a struggle. I heard him tell her that he wanted us for the money before the boot came down and we were trapped in total blackness.

The whole abduction probably only lasted thirty seconds.

In the darkness of the boot, I was completely hysterical, just sobbing with fear as the car started moving. Charlene wasn't making any sound at all. She lay still beside me, with her arm around me and her face pressed against mine.

'What's happening?' I asked her over and over again. 'What's going on?'

I was terrified but I didn't know what of. I didn't have a clue why he had grabbed us or what might happen. I was a naive little innocent, so when Charlene replied 'He's going to rape us and murder us' I genuinely didn't know what she meant. I knew what killing was, of course, but the word 'rape' meant nothing to me.

The worst things that had happened to me were my brother and sister stealing money from my penny pot or borrowing my clothes, or messing up my bedroom, which I hated. Whatever rape might be, I knew that I didn't want to be murdered. I sobbed my heart out, scared and panicked. Charlene tried to calm me down.

'Just keep quiet,' she said. 'Don't worry. We'll be okay.'

She stroked my hair then she started singing to me, a Sade song called 'Your Love is King'. It was very stuffy in the boot and it smelled of petrol and old rubber. There was a picnic rug beneath us with a scratchy texture. The man who had grabbed us put the car stereo on at some point and we could hear a DJ nattering away, but Charlene still kept singing quietly to me until my sobs subsided into a kind of hiccupping. I clung on to her, and I clutched my schoolbag and I began to wonder what everyone at school would think. What would they say when our names were read out at registration and we weren't there?

'I just wanna go to school,' I moaned.

'We'll be back there soon,' she comforted me in a whisper. 'It'll be fine.'

But wherever the man was taking us, it certainly wasn't to school. The journey went on for ages and soon it seemed as though we had been driving for hours and hours. I became worried that there wasn't enough air and we might suffocate. We were cramped together very tightly and my leg began to go to sleep. We were shunted around every time the car turned left or right, or braked and came to a stop then started up again. After a while there was a different sensation, a feeling as though he had driven off the smooth road and onto a crunchy surface like gravel. I started to moan with fear and Charlene said 'Shhh'.

The car stopped and we heard his door slam then seconds later the boot opened and daylight flooded in. Charlene and I cowered away from him, blinking hard. He grabbed hold of her coat and yanked her upwards.

'Out you get!' he said. 'I need to have a chat with you.'

She climbed out of the boot, with him holding tightly onto her. I lay still, completely terrified, unable to utter a word.

'You stay there,' he said. 'I'll talk to you later.' Charlene caught my eye and gave me a worried look then he slammed the boot closed and I was back in the pitch dark again.

I began to moan to myself, tears streaming down my cheeks. Being left on my own was the worst thing I could imagine. If I had Charlene there, I could just about cope but without her I knew I would fall apart.

'Please, please, please let her come back,' I said over and over again in my head.

I heard the car door opening and felt the car sink down as they both got in, then I heard the murmur of their voices inside. His voice was louder. He was asking her questions but I couldn't hear the answers because she was speaking very quietly.

At one point I heard him asking her address. Maybe she'll talk him into taking us home, I thought. Or we could ask him to drop us off at school.

Then I had another thought. Perhaps he would let her go and hang onto me. It was me he had been following that morning before I even met up with her. It was me he'd been after. If I was left on my own with him, I didn't know what I would do. I began to cry even harder, my whole body shaking and my eyes stinging with the floods of tears.

'Please come back, Char,' I sobbed out loud. 'Please don't leave me.'

4
Tuesday late morning

Charlene

When I climbed out of the boot, I saw we were on a stony path in the middle of a big grassy field. I couldn't see any houses but I could hear the rumble of cars nearby, and I got the impression that maybe there was a motorway just beyond the trees. I looked all the way around to see if there was another human being in sight that I could shout to, but there was no one. It didn't occur to me to try to run away. I wouldn't have dreamt of leaving Lisa on her own and anyway, there was nowhere I could have run to out there. He would have caught me before I'd gone a hundred yards.

The man put his arm around me and guided me to the back door of the car, opened it and pushed me in. He climbed in himself and then lifted me up so I was sitting sideways on his lap. I looked at him properly for the first time and saw he had a thin face with a big rough grey moustache and white hair with streaks of brown or black in it. He was wearing a green waxed jacket, like a Barbour or a fisherman's jacket.

'What's your name?' he asked. He sounded very calm

and was speaking in that clear tone of voice that grown-ups use when they're talking to children.

I was too scared not to answer him. 'Charlene.'

'How old are you, Charlene?'

'Ten.'

He patted my knee. 'Good girl. I just want to find out a few things about you so I can get to know you.' He smiled a creepy smile and I looked away.

'What's your favourite colour, Charlene?'

I hated him saying my name but still I answered: 'Green.'

'I bet you're a clever girl. What subjects do you like at school.'

'English.'

He asked more questions about my favourite foods, favourite drinks, favourite toys, and I gave him one-word answers in a low voice, feeling very uncomfortable about sitting on his lap. I didn't ask him his name or what he wanted with Lisa and me. I wasn't feeling at all brave. I had had some bad experiences in my life with the kind of men who like young girls to sit on their laps and they made me very wary of any men I didn't know.

When I'd lived with Auntie Vera and Uncle Harry, I'd been very happy except for one thing. Uncle Harry had a friend called Bert, who was in and out of the house all the time, doing DIY jobs or visiting Uncle Harry, and sometimes he would babysit for me – occasions that I came to dread.

One night I was having a bath and Bert came into the bathroom to watch.

'Do you want to play a fun game?' he asked. 'My sisters and I used to play it all the time.'

'What game?' I asked.

'It's called "Simon says". If I say "Simon says touch your head," you have to touch your head. But if I just say "Touch your head," you don't. You only do it when Simon says. Get it?'

'Yeah.'

'OK. Simon says put your legs up in the air.'

So I did.

'Wave them around.'

I waved them around.

'Hah!' he said. 'You got it wrong. I didn't say "Simon says wave them around."'

I was determined to get it right next time, so when he said 'Simon says touch in between your legs,' I did. And that's how our game started.

He used to tell me how pretty I was, and how funny and clever I was, and I liked hearing that. If I told a joke, he would laugh really hard as if it was the funniest thing in the world. If I told him I'd got a good mark at school, he said he was really proud of me. I liked having him around and at first I didn't realise that what he was doing with me wasn't normal behaviour. After all, Uncle Harry and Auntie Vera were sometimes downstairs at the time, so surely it must be alright. I didn't notice that he always jumped back and stopped our games if he heard their footsteps on the stairs.

The games went further. Bert liked to touch me, kiss me and lick me between my legs, which I thought was a bit yucky, but I let him because he'd get huffy if I didn't. He wanted me to sit on top of him in the bath and have a pee, but I refused point-blank to do that. And sometimes he'd just make me sit naked in front of him with my legs open.

As I got a bit older, I got more and more uncomfortable about our 'games' and I grew to hate Bert and the things he made me do. One day I threatened to tell Auntie Vera about them.

'No one will believe you,' he snapped. 'You're just a slag, like your Mum.'

I gasped, shocked and wounded. I already knew that people called Mum a slag because of all the boyfriends she had. Could it be true that I was one as well? Was this my fault? After that, I didn't dare tell Auntie Vera, but I began to loathe Bert more and more for what he made me do. Sometimes he poked me really hard with his finger and hurt me. Sometimes he got his horrible, smelly penis out and tried to make me touch it, but I refused.

When he wanted me to do something to him, he'd be full of compliments about how pretty my new haircut was, or telling me he liked the colour of my dress; but if I said 'no' to something he wanted me to do, I was a slag, and dirty and no boys would ever want to go out with someone like me. He played mind games and I fell for them. I'd had so many changes in my young life that I just wanted to be loved. I was confused and vulnerable and that's why he targeted me in the first place. It was easy to manipulate a young girl who didn't know what normal family life was like and who yearned to be accepted.

Perhaps the worst thing, though, was when my mum died. For some reason, Bert came along with us to the funeral. All I could think about for the entire time was him sitting there and how much I hated him. It ruined the funeral for me. I couldn't even cry. My big sisters Carol and Rose were next to me and they were sobbing but I couldn't even think about Mum or the fact she was dead because of Bert being there.

I hated Bert more than anybody in the world. I might only be a child but I knew that he was a sick and evil man. When I left Auntie Vera's house to live with my dad, I hoped I would never have to see him again.

Now, sitting in the back of the turquoise car on my abductor's lap, I guessed this man was going to be the same. He had the same sleazy air about him, the wheedling tone, trying to pretend to be nice while his hungry eyes kept staring at me.

'I'm not going to hurt you,' he said. 'It's just that I need some cash so I'm going to ask your mum and dad for ransom money before I take you back.'

'My mum's dead,' I told him.

'I'm sorry to hear that,' he said in a really sympathetic voice. 'Do you live with your dad, then? What's his name?'

'Keith Lunnon,' I said.

He reached into his pocket and took out a little notebook and pen, then got me to spell out our surname. 'What's his address? So I can send him the ransom note.'

I told him my address, then I said, 'Why don't you

phone him? He could get the money for you quicker if you phoned.'

'Good idea,' he said, and took down my phone number, then closed the notebook. 'Thank you, Charlene. You're a good girl. I kidnapped a girl once before for three hours and I nearly got lots of money. But then I got caught and had to go to prison, so this time I'm going to make sure it works.'

He jiggled his knees so I bounced a little bit.

'Can I go back to Lisa now?' I asked. I could hear the sound of her crying in the boot.

He stared at me for a while and I couldn't read his expression but finally he said, 'Yes, why not? We've got plenty of time.'

We got out of the car and he marched me back round to the boot. Lisa's face was bright red and her eyes were huge and swollen with crying. I climbed in beside her and put my arm around her then he shut the boot on us again.

Lisa

As soon as Charlene was back in the boot beside me and the lid was shut, I whispered to her, 'What did he want?'

'He just asked me questions,' she said.

'What kind of questions?'

'He wanted to know where my dad lives so he can get some ransom money. I think he's going to phone him.'

That sounded like good news. If he spoke to Keith,

this would all get sorted out and we'd be able to go back to school. The engine started and the car was moving again, scrunching back across the gravelly path, then it turned right on to a smoother road.

'Did he say where he's taking us?' I asked.

'No.'

Charlene was being very quiet and I wondered if there was something she wasn't telling me, maybe because she was trying to protect me.

'What's he like?'

'Shhh. He might hear us.' She snuggled up to me, pressing her face against mine. 'Just keep quiet and we'll be fine.'

Once again, we seemed to be driving for a long time, although it was probably quicker than the first journey from Cornfield Terrace. When we stopped, I felt him get out of the car and then heard the sound of some doors closing before he opened the boot.

I blinked and tried to focus. We were in a dimly lit room.

'You this time.' He pointed at me.

I tried to shrink back and hide behind Charlene, but he grabbed hold of my arm and pulled me out. I was wearing clogs and they fell off, clattering back into the boot.

'My shoes!' I protested.

'You won't need them,' he said, producing a large holdall, like a sports bag. 'Get in here.'

'No way!' I said, but he grabbed me and started pushing me inside. I realised we were in a garage. It had bare brick walls and the same kind of things that you find in lots of people's garages: a lawnmower, tools, a garden hose hanging on the wall.

'It won't be for long,' he said. 'Just till I get you inside the house.'

'What about me?' Charlene asked in a tiny voice.

'Don't worry. I'll come back for you,' he said, then he slammed the lid of the boot. He shoved me down inside the bag and started to zip up the top.

'I won't be able to breathe!' I panicked. 'You might kill me.'

'It's only for less than a minute,' he said calmly. 'You'll be fine.'

I was all curled up inside and when he lifted the handles of the bag, it was really uncomfortable, squeezing my arm back the wrong way and hurting my shoulder. I tried to wriggle into a better position but it was impossible because we were moving and the bag was swinging to and fro. I heard the garage door open and close then I heard him unlock the door to the house and close it behind him, and finally he put the bag down and unzipped the top.

I clambered out of the bag, desperate to be free of it. Panting a bit, I looked around. We were in a kind of sitting room, as far as I could tell, and it seemed like an old person's room, with all those dingy brown colours they seem to like. The carpet was dark and there was a brown sofa with a table in front of it. It was dim inside the room, because the beige curtains at the patio doors were drawn. In the far corner, there was a dining table and chairs.

The man sat down on the sofa and pulled me over

so that I was standing in front of him, then he started taking my quilted jacket off. I let him do that, but then I jerked away when he tried to pull my school jumper over my head.

'What are you doing?' I asked.

He didn't reply, but stood up and grabbed my jumper again, yanking it over my head. Then he caught the waistband of my skirt and pulled it down.

'Why are you doing this?' I was shaking with fear.

'I told your friend Charlene,' he said quietly. 'I'm holding you for ransom. I want money from your parents.' All the time, he kept taking my clothes off, item by item: my skirt and then my tights.

'My mum and dad will give you anything you want. Just speak to them,' I begged. 'I'll give you their number.'

I only had my shirt and knickers on now and I was hugging myself, trying to stop him looking at me. 'I should be at school by now. I'm going to get into trouble when they find out I'm not there.'

He unbuttoned my shirt and pulled it off, then he pulled down my white cotton knickers. I tried to hold my hands in front of me, but he didn't want that. He caught hold of both my arms and pulled them up over my head, where he held them with one hand. With the other, he picked up my tights and looped them around my wrists then tied them in a tight knot. When he released my wrists, my hands dropped back behind my head and rested on my neck. I couldn't move them, except to raise them. Finally, he lifted me onto his lap so that I was sitting sideways.

‘That’s better now,’ he said.

Better for who? I thought, but I was too scared to say it. My arms ached, my wrists were sore where my tights were knotted around them, and I felt horribly exposed and vulnerable sitting on his lap. I could feel the texture of his trousers under my legs and see his suede lace-up boots tapping on the ground. When he pulled me close, his chequered sweater felt scratchy against my chest. He was staring at my naked body, his eyes darting about and his breath coming rapidly. It was creepy, so I tried to distract him by talking to him.

‘You might get into trouble for doing this. If you drop us back at school for quarter past three, we’ll just come out as normal and then my mum and dad will never know and everything will be fine.’

‘What’s your name?’ he asked.

‘Lisa Hoodless.’

‘And what’s your address?’

I told him, and he pulled out a notebook and wrote it down.

‘Do you want my phone number as well?’ I recited it. ‘Why don’t you phone my mum? She’ll be at home just now.’

He put the notebook down on the table. ‘What’s your favourite food, Lisa?’

‘Pizza and chips,’ I said. ‘Or sausages.’

‘What films do you like?’

‘Why are you asking me this?’

‘I just want to get to know you a little bit. I want to find out what you like.’

He put his fingers between my legs and started stroking me there. At once, I froze. I had no idea what he was doing or why but it felt wrong. Then I knew I had to stop him. I found my voice.

'Stop doing that! I don't like it. Please stop.' I wriggled in his lap but he didn't stop. I looked into his eyes. With most people, you can see a lot in their eyes: their mood, their frame of mind or their emotions. But with this man, there was nothing there – just emptiness, as if there wasn't a real person behind them. I could tell there was no kindness there, and that he didn't care a jot about me.

I felt incredibly confused about the whole thing. Why was I sitting naked on his lap answering questions? What did he want from me? I'd never seen or heard of anything like this in my whole life and couldn't imagine why a strange man would want to do this to me.

'Please stop,' I kept saying. 'I don't like it. Please leave me alone.' I was such a well brought-up girl that I never forgot my pleases and thank yous, even in such a terrifying situation.

I don't know how long he continued looking at me and touching me but it seemed to last for ages and all the time he was asking me questions about my favourite subjects at school, favourite toys, all that kind of thing. I knew that his questions were just a ruse to keep me calm so he could carry on stroking me, but I was far too scared not to answer them, even though I hated it. At last, he stopped, lifted me off his lap onto the sofa and stood up.

'I'll be back in a minute,' he said. 'You stay right there. Don't dare move, because I'll be checking up on you.'

He left the room, taking his notebook with him, and I sat still for a moment, listening to the sound of his footsteps going down the hall and then the front door opening. I didn't hear it close again so I leant over and peeped around the door in the direction he had gone. Then I jumped in terror: he was standing at the front door staring right back at me. I sat up straight on the sofa again, looking straight ahead. I had no idea whether he was going outside the house or was waiting outside the door, so I didn't dare get off the sofa. Instead I looked around at the murky room. Light was streaming in from either side of the patio curtains and I could make out that there was a garden beyond but I didn't dare to make a run for it. The patio doors were bound to be locked and even if they weren't, he would catch me soon enough, and goodness knew what he would do then. I was only little and wasn't a very fast runner. Besides, I was naked and my hands were tied up. I couldn't go out like this.

I wondered if there might be a phone somewhere. Surely everyone has a phone, I thought, and looked carefully around the room. There were a few shelves over by the dining room table and a low coffee table in front of me but I couldn't see a phone anywhere. Even if there had been one, how would I have used it with my hands tied behind my head? If I managed to knock the receiver off, I wondered if I would be able to dial 999 with my nose. But it seemed unlikely, and he might hear me trying and get cross. I was scared he might hit me.

What was he going to do with us? Where had he gone?

Had he gone to phone my mum, like I asked him to? I tried to picture what she would be doing at home: probably feeding the baby, or changing her nappy, or winding her. At not yet a year old, little Georgie took up all Mum's attention. I tried to picture what they would be doing at school. Surely Mr Okrainetz would think it was strange that both Charlene and I hadn't turned up? Would he have told anyone? What would they all think? I'd never played truant or anything like that. I never did anything naughty at school, except perhaps talking in class. I was a good little girl.

Suddenly I remembered a time when I was five and had just started reception at primary school. I don't know why, but I was being a little madam and refused to sit down when it was story time. The teacher asked me several times, but I wouldn't. I thought I was being funny, standing up like that, but then the teacher wrote my name on the blackboard, which is what she did when children were naughty, and I burst into tears.

'You wrote my name on the blackboard,' I sobbed.

'Will you sit down now?' the teacher asked, and I dropped down obediently.

I learnt that morning that it definitely didn't pay to be naughty. I kept looking at my name up there on the board and feeling ashamed and I don't think I was ever disobedient in class again. Five years on the memory was still vivid.

At home, my brother James and sister Christine were always in trouble but I was the goody-two-shoes, the one who finished their dinner, did their homework without being asked and kept their bedroom tidy. It wasn't my style to stand up to adults.

I suppose another, more confident child might have tried to make a run for it that day in the dingy brown room, or might have got up and looked around the house for anything that could help them to escape, but I had no idea where my captor had gone or whether he was testing my obedience. Perhaps, if I were good, he would be kind to me and let me go. Perhaps he was waiting outside to pounce on me if I dared to disobey his orders. So I sat timidly, knees huddled up to my chest, waiting patiently. After about twenty minutes or so, the man who had kidnapped me finally came back into the room, untied my hands and told me to get dressed. When my clothes were back on, he pushed me down into the sports bag again.

I did as he said. I wasn't feeling brave. I just wanted to be back with Charlene. It felt safer with her around.

Charlene

When I was left alone in the boot in that garage, I went berserk. I started screaming and kicking out at the lid, trying to break it open. I was terrified. What was he doing to Lisa? Was he going to do it to me next?

I heard footsteps approaching, then the boot opened. The man was staring down at me crossly. 'What's all the noise about?' he demanded.

'I need a wee,' I said. It was true, but that hadn't been why I was shouting. I just wanted him to come and get me so Lisa and I could stick together. I thought he would have to take me into the house to use the toilet, but he had other ideas.

'Here!' He picked up a bucket and threw it at me.

'I don't want a bucket!' I threw it back at him.

'Fine,' he said calmly, and closed the boot again.

'No, wait! Come back!' I screamed, but I heard the garage door close and there was silence outside.

I started crying now and kicking with all my strength to try and force the boot open, but it wouldn't budge. My brain was working overtime trying to think what I could do. Who was this man? What was he going to do with us? Why us? I had a horrible feeling that we were going to die, and I couldn't bear it. It wasn't fair. Not when I was just starting to be happy. It was too cruel. I imagined how devastated Dad would be. It would destroy him. Thinking of him standing over the grave at my funeral set me off crying even harder until my chest was heaving and I was shaking from head to foot.

I knew clearly what death meant. It was only two years since my mum had died, bringing my whole world crashing down. Death was final. The end. I knew that. And trapped in the boot of the turquoise car that morning, I felt sure that I was about to die.

I was trembling when I heard the garage door open and realised he was coming back for me. The boot opened and I saw he was on his own. Had he killed Lisa already?

'Where's Lisa?' I cried. 'What have you done with her?'

'Don't worry,' he said calmly. 'She's fine. She's fine.'

He grabbed my coat to pull me up and I climbed out of the boot. 'Now, you've got to take off your trousers.'

I looked at his dead eyes and I had a good idea of what would happen next. My experience with Bert had taught me what men like this wanted from little girls, but I was so scared that I think I would have done anything he asked. I pulled my trousers down and slipped them off.

'Your knickers as well,' he ordered.

I pulled my knickers off and tried to wrap my coat around my lower half to protect myself, but he just peeled it off me and threw it into the boot.

'Come and sit in the car,' he instructed, leading me round to the back door.

I followed like a lamb. He made me get into the back seat and sit with my back against the door and my legs spread wide. Then he got in as well and closed the door behind him and just looked at me for ages, without saying anything. He didn't touch me, but his eyes were all glazed and staring.

I couldn't look at him. I peered out the window at all the tools hanging on the garage wall. A single light bulb burned up on the roof and it had a fuzzy halo round it. I remembered when Bert used to sit and stare at me at my aunt and uncle's house, but I had never been scared of Bert in the way that I was scared of this weird, creepy man. I had goose pimples all over me, but they were caused by fear rather than cold.

He leant forward and adjusted my legs to give himself a better view. Still he didn't say anything. It made me feel sick, but I was too terrified to speak. I rested my head back against the window, breathing little shallow breaths and trying to pretend I was somewhere else – anywhere but there.

When he had finished looking, he opened the car door and got out, then gestured for me to follow.

'Put your clothes on,' he said, and I obeyed. 'Get back in the boot.'

I didn't ask him any questions. I just got in and lay very still as he closed the boot on me again.

What on earth is going on? I wondered. It seemed so bizarre. This man was obviously crazy to snatch two girls he didn't know from the street and bring them back to his house to look at them and touch them. Why would anyone want to do such a thing? But I knew what to expect from the things that Bert had done to me and although it was sickening and frightening, at least it didn't hurt. I just wished this man would hurry up and finish whatever he wanted and let us go.

At the back of my mind was the terrible fear that he would decide to kill us so that we couldn't tell on him. I prayed he wouldn't hurt us. Was he capable of murder? He looked so ordinary, like a normal man you'd pass on the street. But he'd already been able to throw us in the boot of his car and ignore our fear and Lisa's tears. Perhaps that meant he was capable of anything. I tried to push those thoughts away.

I heard the garage door opening again and the lid of the boot was lifted. He'd brought Lisa back out again in the sports bag and as she scrambled out of it, I could see she had been crying some more. Her face was swollen and shiny with tears. I was so pleased to see her I could have kissed her.

As soon as he closed the lid of the boot, I whispered: 'What did he do to you?'

Her voice was very shaky. 'He took my clothes off and then he touched me down there.'

'Yeah, me too,' I whispered.

The engine was turned on and the car started reversing out of the garage. We lay still, hugging each other. Soon we could feel we were back on the road again. Neither of us said anything but we were both wondering where on earth he was taking us now, and what he was going to do to us next. We were completely in his power. We had no choice but to do as he said.

5

Tuesday afternoon

Lisa

The car went on for a while and then slowed down and turned sharply. We could tell from the echoing sounds outside that we had driven into some kind of underground car park. When he opened the boot, the lights were orange-coloured and I could see some cars parked. I looked all around to see if there were any people I could shout to for help, but it was empty.

'Lisa, you first,' the man ordered, and brought out the dreaded sports bag.

'Where are we?' I asked, but he didn't reply, just grabbed my arm and forced me to get into the bag again. He zipped up the top and I heard him slam the lid of the boot with Charlene inside.

This time I was in the bag for longer and it became really uncomfortable where I was scrunched up against the bottom. My legs hurt where they were bent up to my chest and my back was getting twisted and I was scared he might bump my head on something as the bag swung back and forwards. He was walking up some stairs and I could hear him puffing and panting with the effort. There was a little hole in the bag that I could see out through and I realised we were going up flights of stairs, round and round in the stairwell. We must have gone up four floors altogether.

He put me down on the concrete floor outside the door to a flat and began fumbling with some keys. The cold of the concrete seeped through the nylon base of the bag, freezing my legs and back. Then the door was opened and I was carried inside and put down on a carpet.

He unzipped the bag and pulled me out. I was in a small room, maybe ten feet by ten feet. It had a big old sofa in it, a TV, a single bed in the corner and a small window with the curtains drawn so the light was very dim.

'Sit down,' he said, pointing at the sofa. I obeyed. 'I'm going down to get Charlene now. Don't even think about escaping because the man next door has a big, fierce dog and it will rip you to pieces if you take one step outside.'

I wouldn't have tried anyway. I was so terrified by now that I did what I was told without answering back or even questioning him much.

Before he left, he switched the TV on. It was some kind of talk show about politics, which I watched for a minute then ignored.

I looked around the room. It was cluttered and dirty, with bits of wallpaper peeling off the wall, and there was a strong smell of damp. To me it smelt like boiled cabbage, which I hated, but Dad had told me that's what damp smelt like. I couldn't see clearly because the curtains were closed but with the light that came through, I noticed a sort of glass-fronted cabinet and a shelving unit loaded with books. There appeared to be lots of ornaments all over it but I couldn't make out what they were. The bed in the corner had a bare mattress, and the sofa I was sitting on was an orange colour with stains and rips and cigarette burns all over it. It was filthy. I tried not to touch anything I didn't have to.

I wondered again when people would realise we were missing. Perhaps if the teachers thought we were off ill, it wouldn't be until quarter past three when Mum came to pick me up from school. I didn't have a watch but I guessed it was only late morning by then. It was still bright daylight outside and I knew that at this time of year, it was starting to get dark by the time school finished. When would the man phone our parents to demand the ransom? Would they go to the police? I remembered that kidnappers always warned in the ransom note that you shouldn't go to the police. Would our kidnapper do that?

I heard keys in the door and then he came into the room with a bizarre kind of parcel wrapped in black bin liners. I realised that it was Charlene, who was completely swathed in black plastic, with holes cut out for her nose and eyes. Maybe she had been too big for the holdall. He unwrapped her quickly and then told her to sit down, so she put herself down beside me on the sofa. Our eyes met briefly.

'What's your name?' I asked the man.

'Never you mind. Call me whatever you like,' he said.

There was no expression on his face. He spoke calmly, without any accent I could make out.

'Why have you brought us here?'

'I told you. I brought you for ransom. Don't even think you'll be able to escape from here. Come over to the window.'

He put his arms around us and led us over to look out the window, and when he pulled back the curtains we saw that we were several floors up, at the same height as the treetops. That's all we could see – just a cloudy, greyish-white sky and bare tree branches swaying in the wind. When we looked down there was a rooftop a couple of floors below and we could just make out some shops underneath that.

'You'll never be able to escape through the window because you would break your legs if you fell from that height.'

He led us back to sit on the sofa again. 'The front door is kept locked so you won't get out that way. You just have to sit tight and wait like good little girls until your parents get me the money.'

'Have you phoned them yet?' I asked.

He took a pouch of Golden Virginia tobacco out of a money belt he was wearing and started passing it backwards and forwards from one hand to the other as if he couldn't decide whether to have a smoke or not. 'No, I'll do it later.'

'Can't you do it now? Please? They'll be worried otherwise.'

'I said later. Not now.' He looked at the sleeves of

Charlene's jumper, which were all raggedy. She had a thing about eating her jumpers. 'It doesn't look as though your family's got much money, sending you to school in a jumper like that.'

'They haven't got a lot,' she said quickly, 'But they'll find whatever you want if you just let us go.'

'I'm not sure what I'm going to do with you,' he said, 'I'll have to decide.' He sat staring from one to the other of us, and in the background the TV was blaring away with men talking about money and things. I was thinking that he must be mad. Who would do something like that? If you were going to kidnap someone, surely you would choose someone rich? Why us?

'I need a wee,' I said after a while.

He looked annoyed but he seemed to realise that there was nothing to be done about it and said grumpily, 'Alright, I'll take you.' He turned to Charlene. 'Stay there. Don't move a muscle.'

He led me out of the room into the hallway and I saw there were four or five doors leading off it. The one on the left was a tiny bathroom with a bath, a sink and a toilet. It didn't look very clean to me. I waited for him to leave the room so that I could pee but he wasn't moving.

'Go ahead,' he said. 'I'm not leaving you on your own.'

I was really desperate by now so I just had to wee with him watching. When I'd finished he handed me a piece of toilet paper, then I flushed and washed my hands and dried them on a manky old towel that was hanging there.

We went back through to the front room. He had

brought our school bags up from the car with him and he opened them and had a quick look through the contents: our lunchboxes, school books and pencil cases. Charlene's bag was a really nice kind of knitted rucksack that her aunt had made for her with lots of different colours in it. Mine was my pink Spice Girls one.

'If you get hungry, you can eat your lunches,' he said.

Charlene and I looked at each other. I didn't feel hungry at all. I felt sick. Neither of us said anything so he just put the bags down beside the sofa then he started pacing around from one room to the next.

We sat still on the sofa staring at the telly, and when he went out of the room for a minute I whispered, 'You OK?' but he came back in again before we could say much. We didn't want to talk in front of him or let him overhear.

Every time he was in another room, I was straining to hear whether he was making the phone calls to our parents but I never heard him talking. Eventually I plucked up the courage and asked, 'Are you going to ring our families now?'

'My plans have backfired a bit,' he said. 'I don't know what to do now. Maybe I should just let you go.'

'OK,' we both said eagerly.

I continued. 'If you let us go, we promise we won't tell the police or anything. We won't even tell our parents. We'll just go home as if nothing has happened.'

'Yeah,' Charlene said. 'You could drop us somewhere round the corner or down the hill and we could walk back. You don't need to drop us at our front doors.'

We got really excited thinking about this, but he just said he had to think about it some more and walked out of the room again.

I don't know how long he paced about the flat while we sat on the sofa, but I guessed it was getting later because eventually kids' programmes came on the telly and I didn't think that happened till about four o'clock.

'Our dads will probably be out looking for us by now,' I whispered. The idea cheered us up. If he wouldn't take us home, surely our parents would find us.

'Do you think they'll go together?' Charlene asked.

I screwed up my nose. 'Probably not. They'll probably spread out.'

We sat and watched some cartoons and then Charlene said she was going to eat her lunch, so I opened mine as well.

'What kind of sandwich have you got?' she asked. 'I've got ham.'

'I've got turkey,' I told her. 'Can I have a bit of your ham one?'

'Do you want to swap? I don't mind.'

We swapped sandwiches and ate each other's, then we drank our juice and ate our crisps as well. Mum had put in my favourite flavour of crisps, which was cheese and onion.

We could hear that the man was in another room. There were muffled thumps as though he was moving things around.

'Are you scared?' I whispered to Charlene.

'Not really,' she said.

'Why not?' I was amazed because I was very scared. It didn't occur to me that she might be trying to be brave for my sake.

'I know what he's going to do with us,' she said, 'because there was a man called Bert at my aunt and uncle's house who used to do stuff like that to me.'

'What kind of stuff?' I had no idea what she meant.

She seemed embarrassed. 'Oh, you know. Just wanting me to take my clothes off and touching me and stuff. It was disgusting.'

'Didn't you tell your aunt and uncle?'

She shook her head. 'I didn't think they would believe me. He was a friend of my uncle's and people never believe children, do they?'

I thought about it. I'd never been in a similar situation so I couldn't say, but I agreed with her. 'I suppose not. Did you tell him you didn't want to do it?'

'Yeah, all the time. I hated it. That's partly why I wanted to come down and live with my dad – to get away from him.'

'Did you tell your dad about it?'

'No. I've never told anyone before. You're the first.'

It was dark outside now and the only light in the room came from the flickering of the TV but I could make out that she had tears in her eyes, so I reached over and gave her a hug. We hugged for quite a while until we heard his footsteps in the hall and we sprang apart as the door opened.

'OK, Charlene, I need you to come with me. Lisa, you're staying here.'

He was holding a couple of pairs of women's tights, in that kind of caramel-beige shade that old ladies wear. 'Put your hands over your head,' he told me and I did what he asked.

He used one of the pairs of tights to tie my hands together behind my head, then he tied my ankles together with the other, pulling the knot so tight that my ankle bones dug into each other and I cried, 'Ouch!'

'You're not to move until we get back,' he said to me. I nodded meekly.

As Charlene left the room with him, she turned round quickly to look at me and I saw from her face that she was scared after all. In fact, she looked petrified. I wished there was something I could do to help her but I couldn't think of a single thing.

Charlene

As he led me into his bedroom, my feet felt like lead and I had a big lump in my throat. This was it. It was going to be horrible. I swallowed hard.

He held my shoulders, guiding me until I was standing beside the bed, then he started taking my clothes off. I stood still, not helping him but not struggling either.

'Just relax, Charlene,' he said. 'I won't hurt you, I promise. It's going to be easier with you because you're bigger than Lisa. Lie down on the bed.'

I lay down carefully on my back, with my legs pressed tightly together. He took off his own clothes. His chest was pale and so skinny you could see his ribs. I didn't look any lower down. When he lay down beside me, he smelled sweaty and dirty and his breath stunk of stale cigarettes.

He got a tub of Vaseline or something from beside the bed and started rubbing it between my legs. I just let my mind go blank and distant, the way I used to with Bert. I tried to think of my hamster, Fluffy, and the cute way she wrinkled her nose. Then I thought about the new bedroom Dad had made for me with the lovely yellow bed with an orange swirly border. My dad had spoiled me rotten since I came to live with him. He kept grinning and hugging me as if he couldn't believe his luck.

He'd been applying to the authorities for custody of me for years, and finally, when I was about nine and a half, they said I could choose where I wanted to live, either at Auntie Vera's or with my dad in Hastings. I said straight away that I wanted to go with Dad. I would miss Auntie Vera but I couldn't stay in that house with Bert coming round all the time, and I thought it sounded nice to live by the sea. Dad was engaged to a woman called Philomena, who had a fifteen-year-old daughter called Ceri-Jane. They were both very nice to me when I visited and just before I moved down I got to be a bridesmaid at Dad and Philomena's wedding, which was lots of fun.

For the wedding, I wore a gorgeous white dress over a red underskirt that showed at the bottom, and a red and white flower headband. I was very nervous at the beginning because I had to walk into the church first, in front of Philomena, and everyone turned around to look at me, but as soon as that was over, I relaxed and enjoyed myself. I loved the party afterwards, where there was dancing and a buffet just loaded with food that I could help myself to whenever I wanted. For the party I got changed into a red sparkly dress with sparkly little shoes and I felt very special. It was the first wedding I'd ever been to.

I tried to keep my mind focused on all the happy images of the wedding day, but the man was lying on top of me now, squashing me. Suddenly he tried to ram himself between my legs and I screamed at the top of my lungs. The pain was unbearable.

'No! Stop! Please don't!'

He put his big hand over my mouth and carried on trying to push himself inside me and I struggled in complete panic, finding it hard to breathe. His hand was covering my nose as well and I really thought I was about to suffocate or have an asthma attack. I tried to signal to him with my eyes that I couldn't breathe but his expression was blank and staring as he concentrated on what he was trying to do.

Bert had never done anything like this. The pain went on and on. Once he moved his hand from my mouth, I started pleading and pleading with him to stop, tears streaming down my face. I tried everything I could think of.

'If you stop now, I'll never tell anyone. I'll get my dad to give you anything you want. Please stop, please. I'm asthmatic. I might die.'

The intensity of the pain made it hard to cut myself off from what was happening, but I tried to think about my dad's kind, loving face and how he was bound to be out looking for me by now. I prayed to God that he would find me soon.

Then, he did stop. He got off me and went out of the room. I curled up into a little ball and listened as he crossed the hallway to the sitting room. I heard him say a few words to Lisa and then he was back, making me lie flat and climbing on top of me so he could start stabbing away with his willy again. I closed my eyes so I wouldn't have to look into his horrible face.

There was a clock on the bedside table and I could hear it ticking but I couldn't see it while I was squashed up underneath that man with his ribs sticking into me and his horrible panting breath in my ear. I think he kept trying for about an hour, then he gave up. He seemed frustrated, as though it wasn't working out the way he wanted it to. He pulled me on top of him then and made me lie there for ages without saying anything. His chest was heaving up and down with the efforts he'd been making.

Now, I felt numb. Between my legs it was agony but I'd stopped crying and I'd closed down, like I did when I heard that Mum had died. I let my mind go fuzzy and tried not to think about things or let them touch me. I told myself this wasn't the worst thing that had ever happened to me in my life. Mum dying was far, far worse, and I survived that so I would survive this too.

Finally he lifted me off him and gave me a baggy t-shirt to put on. We walked through to the sitting room where

Lisa was still on the sofa, all tied up. Someone was screaming on the TV programme and he switched it off. The silence right afterwards was horrible. Lisa was looking up at me but I couldn't meet her eye. I just sat in the corner of the sofa and pulled my knees up to my chest.

He untied Lisa, gave her a t-shirt and told her to change into it. Then he brought us a smelly old quilt and threw it over us.

'Time to go to sleep,' he said. 'You can sleep together on the sofa if you top and tail. No more talking now.'

He left the room, closing the door behind him and switching off the light.

'Are you OK?' Lisa whispered in a tiny voice.

'Yeah,' I said.

'I heard you crying. What did he do?'

I took a deep breath. 'He raped me.'

There was a long pause then Lisa's little voice asked, 'What's rape?'

She didn't know. I'd known what rape was since as far back as I could remember. At my Mum's house, she had let me watch eighteen-certificate films on the telly – whatever she was watching with her mates – and I'd seen everything in graphic detail.

I explained to Lisa about how the man puts his willy inside you and she seemed stunned. She couldn't imagine how such a thing was possible and I had to assure her that it was.

'So did that man put his thing inside you?' she asked.

'I don't think he could get it in, but he tried. It really hurts.'

'Oh my God! That's horrible!'

We heard him walking about in the hall so we were quiet for a bit then I realised that Lisa was nodding off to sleep so I kicked her.

'Don't! We mustn't sleep. You have to stay awake.'

She tried her best but I could tell even in the dark that she kept slipping off and I'd kick her again. I don't know why I wanted her to stay awake. I just didn't want to be left on my own.

When I was seven or eight, I used to have nightmares about a film called *It* that I'd seen back at Mum's. Based on a Stephen King novel, it was about an evil clown who comes back to life every thirty years and murders the children of the town. In one scene, the clown comes up through the toilet and because of that I was nervous about going to the toilet in places I didn't know. I hadn't yet had a wee in our abductor's flat.

For years, I had to turn the faces of my teddies round before I went to sleep so that I wouldn't wake up to find any of them looking at me, and I had to get someone else to turn the light off once I was in bed because I couldn't put my foot on the floor in the dark in case there was something lurking down there.

I kicked Lisa again and hissed at her: 'Stay awake,' but she just gave a sleepy murmur. 'Please, Lisa.'

''M trying,' she mumbled, but I could tell she wasn't going to make it. I didn't feel tired at all. Just scared and numb and sad: all those emotions mixed up together.

I remembered how happy I had been when I arrived in Hastings to live, and Dad showed me my new bedroom and let me choose new clothes and things I wanted for the room. At the beginning it had all been lovely. He'd taken me to Phoenix House to show me where he worked and they all made a huge fuss of me and said how lucky he was to have such a gorgeous daughter. But I hadn't realised that he worked really long hours. He was at Phoenix House most weekends and on weekdays he'd leave at seven in the morning to go and work in a prison in Kent, where he did drug counselling, and he wouldn't get back till seven at night. Sometimes it felt as though I hardly saw him.

Lying on the sofa, I had a sudden panic about my hamster. Who would feed Fluffy while I was away? Would someone change her water? Or would they forget all about her? Would I come back to find she had died of starvation?

I tried to picture what they would all be doing at home. Would Ceri-Jane be sitting in front of the telly doing her homework? Would Phil be in the kitchen tidying up the dinner things or would she be watching telly as well? What would Dad be doing?

Suddenly I knew exactly what Dad would be doing. I could picture him so clearly it was spooky, like a premonition. He would be in his car, driving up and down every street in the entire area, one after the other, stopping to search parks and waste ground, leaving no stone unturned until he found me. He probably had a big torch with him. I could picture the concentration on his face and I knew he wouldn't sleep at all that night while his little girl was out there somewhere. If it were possible to find me, my dad would do it because he just wouldn't stop looking until I was found. He would never give up.

With that comforting thought in my head, I finally drifted off to sleep.

6

Wednesday morning

Lisa

I'd been utterly terrified when I heard Charlene screaming in the next room. It sounded as though the man was really hurting her. I thought maybe he was biting her or pinching her, because I couldn't imagine what else would cause that amount of pain.

It was too upsetting to sit there listening to it so I got up from the sofa and hobbled towards the door, thinking that maybe he would stop if we both told him to. It was hard to stagger forwards with my ankles tied together but I made it as far as the sitting room door then I heard him getting up. My courage failed and I dived back to the sofa and was sitting down again by the time he came into the room and looked at me suspiciously. He was stark naked. I looked away, embarrassed.

'What were you doing?' he asked.

'I can't feel my hands,' I said. 'They're really throbbing.'

'Just sit still,' he snapped. 'I don't want any nonsense from you.'

Then he went back to the other room and I heard Charlene screaming and crying some more, and it lasted for ages. I'm next, I kept thinking. Whatever he's doing to her, he's going to do to me.

I'd never experienced violence from an adult. My dad would sometimes smack my brother James when he'd done something bad but he had never so much as raised a finger to me, and Mum would never have dreamed of hitting us. James had beaten me up sometimes, but only in the way that kids do, maybe pinning me down on the floor so I couldn't move, or giving me a dead leg or a Chinese burn on my wrist.

Why would a stranger want to snatch Charlene and me from the street and bring us back to his flat in order to hurt us? It didn't make any sense at all no matter which way I looked at it.

When Charlene came back from her ordeal and explained to me in whispers what rape was, I couldn't get my head round it. How could a man get his willy inside you? I'd seen my brother's willy in the bath when we were younger but obviously it wasn't erect so I didn't understand how that would work at all. And I also couldn't imagine where it would actually go. The whole idea was shocking and revolting, and I dreaded him trying to do it to me. Charlene said that it hurt very badly and I could see she was very upset. She said it was still sore and she kept shifting her position on the sofa, obviously uncomfortable and in pain.

I felt terrible that I couldn't stay awake that night because she wanted company after what she had been through but my eyes kept closing, as if there were lead weights in my eyelids. It was quite warm and stuffy in the room – I suppose there was central heating – and it had been a long day.

The next morning we both woke at the same time and we could hear the man rustling around in one of the other rooms. Then he came in, dressed in the same trousers as the day before but with a different shirt. He was wearing blue sheepskin moccasin slippers, just like ones my dad had, and that freaked me out. He went to the window, opened the curtains and then came to the sofa, knelt down on the floor in front of us and put his head in his hands.

'What have I done?' he asked us, running his fingers through his hair, obviously not expecting an answer. He sounded really upset. 'I'm so sorry. I've got myself into a big mess and I don't know how to get out of it. I should never have taken you.'

Charlene and I looked at each other quickly. Did this mean he would take us home again?

'My name's Alan,' he said. 'This is where I live. The house I took you to yesterday is my parents' place but they've been away in Australia for two months. None of this would have happened if they hadn't gone away.' He covered his face with his hands for a moment, then looked up and stared hard at Charlene.

'Do you really hate me? You must hate me for what I did to you,' he said to her in a pathetic voice.

She didn't answer, but I sensed that his remorse might be a chance for us to get away. 'Why don't you let us go now?' I suggested quickly. 'You could drop us off outside a police station or something and just drive away and they wouldn't catch you.'

'But I want to be caught. I deserve to be caught. I should be in jail. It's a good life in there. You get three meals a day and you don't have to worry about money and bills. I feel safe when I'm in jail.' He looked really sorry for himself, as though he wanted us to sympathise with him.

I felt a chill of fear when I heard this. If he'd been in prison, he must be a very bad person. I didn't dare ask what he'd gone to jail for, but then he told us.

'I kidnapped a girl before, ages ago. She was French. I picked her up at a bus stop and drove her around for a while but when we got out of the car she threw her bag at me and ran away. Then I kidnapped another girl and brought her back to the place where I was living, but someone had seen my car and three hours later the police turned up and arrested me and that's why I went to jail. It was fair enough. I shouldn't have done it.'

'When did you get out of jail?' I asked. Had he just escaped? Perhaps he was on the run from the police.

'Four years ago,' he said. 'I've been good since then – right up until now. If only my parents hadn't gone away, none of this would have happened. Sometimes I just can't handle life on the outside. I'm a bad person, you see.' He looked at both of us, as if wanting us to contradict him, but we didn't say anything.

'You must hate me,' he said. 'Why don't you hit me?'

'I don't want to hit you,' I told him.

'Go on. Slap me!' He moved closer so he was sitting right in front of us. 'I won't mind. Do it really hard.'

I thought it might be some kind of trap and if I slapped him he would slap me back. I didn't want to touch him but he kept going on and on about it.

'Go on, slap me! Please.'

Finally, I swung my hand back and gave him a right whack across the face. He seemed surprised and clutched his cheek.

'Thank you,' he said quietly. 'I deserved that.'

'Why don't you promise us you're not going to do it again?' I suggested, feeling a bit braver. 'If you're nice to us from now on and you drop us off at a police station, we'll tell the police that you treated us well. Then they won't be so hard on you. Do you promise?'

'OK.'

'Honestly?' I looked at Charlene. 'You won't rape either of us again?'

'No, I won't,' he said. He turned to Charlene. 'I'm sorry if I hurt you and I won't do it again.'

'And you'll let us go?' I persisted.

'Yes, later,' he said. 'I just have to get the ransom first.'

'Did you call my dad?' Charlene asked, the first time she had spoken to him that morning. She seemed very wary of him now.

'Yes,' he told us. 'But he says he won't pay. That's why I've got a problem on my hands and I don't know what to do with the pair of you.'

Charlene looked stunned when she heard her dad wouldn't pay.

'Did you phone my parents?' I asked. 'What did they say?'

'They won't pay either.' He was tapping his fingers on the carpet.

My stomach twisted up. I couldn't believe it. My first thought was that he must have asked for too much and they simply couldn't get their hands on the money. 'What did they say?' I asked in a small voice.

'Nothing. Just that they weren't paying.'

But that couldn't be right. I tried to imagine my parents saying they wouldn't pay to get me released and I couldn't. I wondered if maybe they had called the police and the police had told them not to pay. Otherwise it didn't make any sense to me.

'My dad would pay. I know he would,' Charlene said firmly.

'Well, he won't. So, you see, I have to decide what to do with you. But don't worry, girls. I'll think of something.' He stood up. 'You two stay here. I need to think.'

After he left, Charlene whispered, 'I don't believe him. I know my dad would pay. He could borrow money from Auntie Vera if he had to.'

I was pretty sure my parents would pay him as well but I couldn't figure out what was going on. 'Maybe he left a message on the answer machine and they didn't get it?' I hated the fact that he could put even the tiniest seeds of doubt in my head.

'One of them must have heard, and they would tell the others. My dad would ring your mum,' Charlene said, and I knew it was true. She sounded very certain.

'I suppose people at school will know by now,' I said. That was a funny thought. 'Do you think they'll make an announcement at assembly that we've been kidnapped?'

'Yeah, maybe.'

'Everyone will be so worried.'

Charlene giggled. '*Stevie* will be all worried about you.'

I blushed thinking about him. I didn't want him to know about all the things the man had been doing to us, especially to Charlene. 'It's funny,' I said. 'Normally I hate school but right now I really miss it. I wish we were there at this minute with Mr Okrainetz handing out worksheets and kids messing around and us chatting away to all the friends who sit near us.'

'I know what you mean,' she said. 'I'd even be happy to have double science right now. Or PE. If I get out of here, I'm never going to complain about school again.'

That word 'if' made me tremble. Did she think there was a chance we wouldn't get out? 'He said he would let us go later,' I reminded her quietly.

'Yeah, I'm sure he will,' she said, a touch too quickly.

We were silent for a moment, listening to the sounds of him moving around in the bedroom.

'Do you think he's mad?' I asked, picturing the blankness of his eyes and the way they stared at us.

'No, I think he's evil,' she replied with a shiver.

Just after this, I realised I needed a wee but I couldn't face going on my own and coming across him out in the hall. I was still only wearing his t-shirt and my school clothes had disappeared. He must have taken them away during the night. 'Will you come to the loo with me,

Char?' I pleaded. I suddenly realised that she hadn't even been since we got there. 'Don't you need to as well?'

'I hate going to loos I don't know,' she said. 'Besides, I'm so sore down there I think it would sting.'

'Just come with me then? Please?'

She got up and we held hands as we went out the door to the hallway.

'What do you think you're doing?' he snarled. We jumped and turned to see him sitting in front of a computer in a room I hadn't seen before, full of papers scattered all over the place.

'We just need to go to the toilet,' I told him.

He stood up and we cowered back against the wall as he came towards us. 'Come on then, hurry up,' he said. He led us into the bathroom and stood watching as I had a wee. When I finished, he tore off a sheet of loo paper and handed it to me. Charlene refused to go and I wondered how on earth she could hold it for so long. I suppose we hadn't had much to drink in the last twenty-four hours – just the juice from our lunchboxes.

'Back you go,' he said. 'I've got a lot to do. And no talking this time. Don't think I can't hear you.'

His voice was much less friendly than it had been earlier on when he wanted us to forgive him. He was giving us orders again and staring at us with those mean little eyes. We never knew where we were with him from one moment to the next.

Back in the sitting room, we sat on the sofa, whispering about what we were going to do when we got out. I said

I wanted to see my granddad as soon as I got home. Charlene wanted to give her dad a hug and then she said she would play with her hamster, Fluffy.

Suddenly the door opened and he came in and stood in front of us, staring at us in a peculiar way as if making a decision.

'You're too little,' he said to me at last. 'I don't think it would work. So I'm going to take Charlene into the bedroom again.' He reached out his hand to pull her up from the sofa. She gave a little cry of fear and tried to wrestle her hand away, but he was so much stronger she had no choice but to stand up.

'But you promised you wouldn't!' I cried, appalled at his reversal. 'A promise is a promise.'

He ignored me.

'Stop! You mustn't do it!' I said. 'We'll tell the police on you.'

Charlene was looking at me and her face was white with terror. I could see that she was trembling. I gave her a look that said 'Sorry.' What else could I do? Even if we both fought him with all our strength, we didn't stand a chance.

He switched the TV on, then dragged Charlene with him out of the sitting room. I felt a mixture of relief that it hadn't been me and a terrible sense of guilt. It wasn't fair that she should get raped just because she was bigger, but what could I do? He was skinny but he was tall and strong. He was a grown man. Poor Charlene. Poor, poor Char.

I pulled my knees up to my chest and hugged them as

tightly as I could, just waiting and listening, my heart pounding and my ears buzzing. Before long I heard the sound of her screaming, 'No, please stop!' and I squeezed my arms over my ears to try and block it out.

In the background, the television was showing a programme with exercises to help you lose weight. The world was just going on as normal while we were trapped in here. Nothing had changed. I felt angry with everyone who was carrying on their everyday lives as if nothing had happened. Why didn't they come and rescue us? Where on earth were they?

Charlene

I never believed it when he came in to say sorry to us on the Wednesday morning and was acting as if he wanted to be our friend. I knew it was all an act. Did he really think we were so dumb that we would fall for it? I hated him with a passion and I knew by then that he was capable of anything. He didn't care about us in the slightest. Lisa was doing most of the talking because I filled up with hatred whenever I looked at his long face with its bristly moustache and heard his clear, well-spoken voice. Anger and hate were bubbling away inside me, mixed up with a fear that paralysed me, and I couldn't even stand to talk to him.

When he took me back into the bedroom for the second time, he began by trying to convince me that he was a good person.

'I'm being nice and gentle with you, aren't I?' he asked, as he rubbed the Vaseline onto me. He had taken off the t-shirt I'd slept in so I was naked again. 'If you were with my neighbour next door, he'd be rough and really hurt you. He wouldn't bother with lubrication. He'd probably rip you to pieces.'

I ignored him and turned my head away. The bedroom was small and dark, with the curtains permanently drawn even in daytime. There was a double bed with a dirty, thin quilt on it, and a tall wooden wardrobe. I screwed up my eyes and thought I could see our school clothes and shoes on top of the wardrobe. We would need these if we tried to escape some time – but I hoped it wouldn't come to that. Surely everyone would be out looking for us by now. If Alan had phoned my dad about the ransom maybe they would be able to trace where the call came from – I'd seen that in the movies. They must know in which area it was made, at least.

When he'd finished smearing me with Vaseline, he climbed onto me, crushing me with his weight and puffing and grunting in my ear. I screamed in agony as he started trying to rape me again. The pain was worse than the day before because I was already sore down there but he was still thrusting away like mad, pushing as hard as he could. I tried to distance myself the way I used to with Bert but the constant ramming against my sore, swollen flesh made it difficult.

Why was he doing this to me? Would he ever try it on with Lisa or was it going to be me the whole time? It wasn't my fault I was bigger. I could see what he meant, though. If he was having so much trouble raping me, it would never work with Lisa because she was much smaller. I didn't think she would be able to handle it at all.

When Mum died, Auntie Vera told me that she had gone to heaven and would be watching over me from there, like a guardian angel. I wondered if she was watching me at that moment. Wasn't there something she could do? A sign she could give? I knew ghosts couldn't ring the police but if she could just make something topple over and crash to the ground that might distract him and make him stop.

I believed in heaven, and that Mum was somewhere up there, but I'd always had trouble accepting the idea of a God with white robes and a long flowing beard. Nothing about it made sense. I could see that there were bad things in the world, things like wars, massacres and plane crashes. If God was all-powerful and he didn't stop them, then he wasn't a very nice God. Most of all, if there was a God, why didn't he stop this man raping me? Why would he let that happen? I was just a little girl, I didn't deserve this and I was powerless to stop it on my own.

I thought that but, inside my head, I was praying as I lay there on that bed: Please God, let us be found soon because I can't take much more of this. Over and over again, I breathed, 'Please, God, please, God, please, God.'

Eventually he stopped and lay panting beside me. I wouldn't talk to him or cuddle him back when he cuddled me. It was my only rebellion.

'Be nice,' he pleaded, signalling to me to roll over into his arms. 'Come here.'

I wouldn't co-operate. He had to pull me over, while I held myself stiff as a board. I hoped he could feel the hatred flowing out of my pores and burning out of my eyes. I wished I was brave enough to swear at him and call him all the worst names I could think of but I was far too scared of him. I couldn't bear any more pain.

'That's enough,' he said after a while. 'Let's go and fetch Lisa.'

I started to get up.

'No, stay there,' he said. 'Don't move.'

He disappeared next door and when he came back, he was pushing Lisa in front of him.

'You OK?' she mouthed at me, and I shook my head slightly, tears coming to my eyes.

'Lie down beside her,' he instructed, so Lisa lay down facing me. He took her t-shirt off so we were both naked, then he tied our hands above our heads. Mine were tied with a piece of cloth or something and it really dug into my wrists like a knife.

We rolled on to our sides to look at each other and tried to ignore him. Our faces were so close together I could feel her breath on my cheek, the way we had been in the boot of the car. He watched us from the foot of the bed for a long while. The silence was spooky. We could hear him breathing heavily but he didn't say or do anything.

When he'd had enough, he said, 'OK, Charlene, you can go and watch TV now.'

I felt guilty about the panic I could see on Lisa's face.

'Don't leave me,' she begged.

'I have to,' I said quietly. 'You'll be OK.'

He pulled me up by the arms and led me back through to the sitting room where I sat down in front of the television set feeling completely numb. I'd lost all the feeling in my hands, the cloth was tied so tightly. I couldn't let myself think about what Lisa might have to go through next door. She must be so scared. Would she scream and cry the way I had?

I'd only got into the boot of the car with her because I wanted to protect her but it had been a huge mistake because of course there was nothing I could do against a grown man. I wondered what I could do to fight him. If there was a knife lying somewhere in the flat, perhaps I could stab him? I looked carefully around the room but there was nothing resembling a knife anywhere. Perhaps there would be one in the kitchen, wherever that was. Would I have the courage if I was facing him and there was a knife in my hand? I wondered how easy it was to stab another person. Where would you aim for? How easily would the knife go in? Of course, I'd have to wait until my hands weren't tied up any more.

Suddenly the blaring music for the news came on and there were pictures of Lisa and me on the screen behind the newsreader's head.

'The search continues for the two Hastings girls missing since yesterday morning,' he said.

I nearly jumped off the sofa in my excitement. The picture they were using of me was one that had been taken in the summer when my dad took me to Butlins. I was wearing a cream-coloured dress and matching hair-band and I was smiling. Lisa's was her school picture, taken the year before.

The newsreader read out the other headlines then came back to us because we were the top story of the day. He said: 'Police in East Sussex are growing increasingly worried about the safety of two schoolgirls missing since yesterday. Charlene Lunnon and Lisa Hoodless were last seen when they set off for the short walk to their school in St Leonards.' According to the report, loads of police officers had been out combing the entire neighbourhood all night long and the army were being called in to help. That was exciting. They showed pictures of policemen with dogs looking in back gardens round our way. I recognised the street they showed.

I wished Lisa could see this. I glanced towards the door but it was firmly shut and I couldn't hear any sound from inside the bedroom.

Then the newsreader said that there was a theory we might have run away to see my sister in London, or possibly to visit my mum's grave. He said there had been a sighting of us on a bus in Plumstead, and that a school friend of ours said I had talked about going to Mum's grave. I wanted to jump up and shout at the screen as if the newsreader would be able to hear me if I was only loud enough. I wanted to yell out that first of all, my mum had been cremated and her ashes were in my sister Rose's front room so how could I have gone to her grave? And secondly, how could we have been seen on a bus in south London when we'd been locked up in this smelly, dark flat the whole time since yesterday morning? The sighting in Plumstead was absolute rubbish and it made me panic because it was sending everyone in entirely the wrong direction.

Why would anyone think we had run away? I wondered. Surely our parents wouldn't believe that. We were obedient little girls, and I was very happy in my new home after all my moving about, so I had no reason to run anywhere. I didn't know either of my half-sisters very well because they were much older than me. Carol was about thirty and Rose was in her twenties so I didn't have much in common with them. They'd be the last people I would run away to see.

The item finished by saying that fears were growing as time passed and then the news moved on to the next story. I felt so frustrated I could have thrown something at the television set. Just stop looking in London, I wanted to yell. We haven't run away! Why hadn't anyone spotted us being bundled into a car in the middle of Cornfield Terrace? I should have dropped something like a hanky to give them a clue, as people did in the movies.

I couldn't wait for Lisa to come out so I could tell her what I'd seen. What would she have to say about it? It was exciting to be on the news, but I was desperately worried that they weren't looking for us in the right place.

Then I heard her screaming, and it was as if a cold hand tightened around my heart. He was trying to do it to her as well. Poor old Lisa. She was too little. It wasn't fair. If only I wasn't tied up I could have gone running in there and started punching and hitting him with all my strength and maybe I could even have found something to whack him over the head with. But I wasn't that brave. I was already struggling to cope and I didn't want to risk provoking him in case it got worse than it already was.

I could smell his smell on me and it wasn't nice. I seemed to be hurting all over, especially my wrists, but in my mind there was a kind of blankness. I sat and stared at the rest of the news programme without hearing a single thing the newsreader said. I watched the pictures without seeing them. At the end of the broadcast they repeated the headline about us but without adding anything new. I listened as if it was about someone else: two other girls who had gone missing, not us.

7
Wednesday lunchtime

Lisa

I started shaking from head to foot as he led Charlene out of the bedroom then came back on his own. 'What are you going to do to me?' I asked.

'Don't worry. I'm not going to do anything.'

I turned the other way so I didn't have to look at his pasty white skin and sticking-out ribs. His willy was sticking out as well and I certainly didn't want to look at that.

'You shouldn't be scared of me,' he said, sitting down beside me. 'I've got lots of friends your age who come to visit me at the flat here and we have a great time. They play computer games and tell me about what they're doing at school. Maybe you could play on the computer later. Would you like that?'

'OK,' I said quietly.

'There's one girl who used to come round most days and I really love her. She's very pretty and such a nice girl.' He stroked the side of my face with his fingers. 'You're pretty too. In fact, you're beautiful.' I pulled away but he just moved closer and carried on stroking my face. 'So you see you shouldn't be scared of me. You'll have a very nice time here. All the children like playing with me.'

'Charlene and I just want to go home,' I told him.

'You will. I'll take you home later. I just want to get to know you a little better first.'

He started stroking my hair and then he untied my hands. I sat up and rubbed my wrists to get the circulation back. 'Why don't you lie down? You'll be much more comfortable.'

'I don't want to lie down.' I wriggled with unease, trying to get away from his stroking hand.

'Go on,' he urged, and he pulled me up the bed, then pushed me down onto the pillows and lay beside me. I could smell his stale, horrible breath and the stink of his armpits.

'Why are you doing this?' I asked him. 'It's not nice to kidnap people and stop them from going home.'

'It's not my fault,' he said. 'If your parents would just pay the ransom you could go straight away.'

'Have you really asked them? Who did you talk to?'

'I talked to your mum. She said it was OK if you stayed here for a while.'

'That's rubbish.' I knew he was lying now. Mum had always told me about not talking to strange men or getting in their cars or anything like that. 'You're lying!'

He was stroking my back. 'Stop it! No!'

'Come on, Lisa.' His hand started to move further down. I pressed my legs firmly together, scared he was going to try to do what he had done to Charlene.

'Please leave me alone,' I begged, trying to wrap myself up in the quilt. Suddenly I started thinking about Nan and Granddad. I wished with all my heart that they were there. They were the people I felt safest with in the world. Even though they had divorced years ago when my mum was a baby, they still got on well and Nan would sometimes pop round to his house while I was there. She was a taxi driver and if she needed a wee when she was out on duty she would just come in to use his loo. I liked it that they were still so friendly.

Alan had got under the quilt and he caught hold of my hand and put it on top of his willy. 'Hold me,' he instructed, but I jerked my hand away, revolted. I couldn't believe he wanted me to touch that thing.

'No, I don't want to.'

'You're so beautiful,' he started telling me again. 'I could really fall for you.' Then he grabbed my hand and tried to force it onto him. We tussled like that for ages, with him grabbing my hand and me saying 'No!' and pulling away and for a while he seemed so pathetic that I almost wasn't scared of him any more.

Then he leaned over for a pot of Vaseline or something and at once I felt scared. I knew what he was going to do now – Charlene had warned me. I was horrified at the thought that he might try and push that thing in me. He smeared the grease over his fingers and then started rubbing it between my legs. I struggled to get away. 'Leave me alone!' I shouted, wanting to cry. 'I'm not going to do it with you. I'm not going to let you rape me.'

It was useless resisting because he was just too strong for me. He rolled on top of me and my nose was squashed up against his chest just near his horrible armpit smell. His skin was all hot and clammy. When he forced my legs apart and put his willy in between them, I screamed blue murder and struggled with all my strength.

'You're hurting me!' I yelled. 'Stop it!'

He paused for a moment and put on more Vaseline.

'Doesn't it hurt you too?' I asked.

'Yeah. A bit,' he said.

'So why are you doing it? Just stop.'

He ignored me and started trying to push it in again so I started screaming the place down. He put his hand over my mouth to shut me up and that was even more terrifying because I really couldn't breathe. I soon realised that I would have to stop struggling and screaming and let him do what he wanted because otherwise I might suffocate. I didn't want to die.

I lay very still after that and kept quiet except when I couldn't stop myself from crying out with pain. He went on trying to force himself into me. Tears were streaming down my cheeks but he completely ignored that. He didn't care about me at all. He wouldn't care if I suffocated. I meant nothing to him.

I made all sorts of promises in my head while I was lying there. If only it would stop and he would let us go, then I wouldn't fight with my brother and sister any more. I'd just let them take my money if they wanted to. I'd never be mean to anyone at school and I'd do all my schoolwork without complaining. I'd stop talking in class. I'd be the perfect daughter and granddaughter and sister and friend. I'd do anything it took just to get out of there.

When he had finished, I could feel sticky stuff all over my tummy. What on earth was that? It didn't feel greasy like the Vaseline. He lay cuddling me and suddenly I felt more angry with him than anything else. I think I could have killed him at that moment if I'd had a gun in my hand. He started telling me I was beautiful again and I completely ignored him, pulling my head away when he tried to stroke my face. At last he let me get up and pull the t-shirt on again and took me back through to where Charlene was sitting on the sofa. When he untied her hands, they were purple with great big grooves on her wrists that looked very sore.

'I'm going to have a bath,' he said. 'You girls stay right there and don't move.'

As soon as he left the room Charlene whispered, 'Are you OK? Did he do it?'

'He tried to. I don't know if he did or not.' I was still a bit puzzled about what exactly happened in rape and unsure about whether that's what he had done to me. 'It really hurt, like you said.'

'Guess what?' She couldn't contain her excitement. 'We were on the telly!'

'Really? What did it say?' I was suddenly filled with hope.

'It was on the news. It said we've been missing since yesterday morning and the police and the army are looking for us. But some idiot at school told them that we were talking about running away to London to go to my mum's grave so they're looking up there.'

'Who would say that? You've never talked about going to your mum's grave.'

'That's because she doesn't even have one.' Charlene

rolled her eyes. 'But I'm just worried that they're looking for us in the wrong place so they won't find us. They said there was a sighting of us on a bus in Plumstead.'

'Maybe we could be in London,' I suggested. 'Not on a bus, obviously, but he was driving for ages so we could be.'

We both thought about that for a while. Charlene got up to have another look out the window but there was nothing to see except bare tree branches and high-rise apartment blocks against a cloudy grey sky. 'If it is London, it's not a bit of London I know,' she said finally.

'I wonder if there's something with his address on it somewhere.' I got up and we both started poking around in all the junk he had left lying about, trying to find a letter or an official form or something that would tell us where we were. There were all kinds of ornaments made out of wood and glass, of little people and animals. Not nice ornaments, though; you wouldn't want them in your own house. They were just junk like you'd find in a jumble sale.

'Let's go and have a look in the kitchen,' I suggested. 'If he asks what we're doing, we could just say we wanted a drink of water.'

'OK, but quietly,' Charlene said.

We crept through to the kitchen, which had beige Formica units, a sink and a cooker and fridge. She started looking in all the drawers while I got two glasses out of a cupboard and ran water into them.

'Look! All the cutlery's gone.' She pointed into the drawer. 'There're only a couple of spoons. He must have hidden the knives and forks in case we attacked him with them.' She opened the drawer below the cutlery one and pulled out a letter. 'Hah!' She showed it to me. 'Alan Hopkinson is his name, and the address is Kingfisher Drive, Eastbourne.'

I went to have a look. Charlene was repeating it to herself quietly, over and over. She whispered, 'I'm memorising it so we can tell the police.'

'Eastbourne's not so far,' I said hopefully. 'It's not even half an hour away in the car.'

I opened the fridge but there was nothing at all inside it. All I found in the cupboards was one sachet of Hot and Sour Cup-a-Soup. It didn't look as though he was planning on feeding us.

There was a splashing sound from the bathroom then we heard the plug being pulled out. He must be getting out of the bath. Charlene put the letter back where she had found it and, clutching our glasses of water, we scurried back through to the sitting room. We were sitting quietly on the sofa when he came in, dressed in a shirt and trousers and those moccasin slippers, his hair all wet and combed down neatly.

'I've decided I'm going to take you home later,' he announced, 'but not until it starts to get dark. What do you want to do this afternoon? Do you want to play a computer game?'

'OK,' I said hesitantly. I didn't want to accept any favours from him, but I thought that maybe there might be more clues in the computer room about who he was and why he had taken us.

'Come on then.' He held out his hand to me. Charlene stood up as well but he said, 'No, you have to come through one at a time.'

I didn't want to go on my own but he took my hand and pulled me out through the hall to the computer room. It was tiny, like a box room, and it was full of cardboard boxes and piles of papers and junk. I was peering around trying to see if there was a telephone – surely he must have a phone somewhere in the flat – but I couldn't see one. He switched the computer on and it flickered to life but it was a very old one with a black-and-white screen and the keyboard was filthy. He sat down in front of it then lifted me so that I was sitting on his lap, which I hated. I squirmed to try and get off.

'We won't be able to play together if you don't sit on my lap,' he said, 'because I don't have another chair. I've got a Tarzan game. My son loves playing Tarzan with me.'

'Are you married?' I asked timidly.

'Yes.'

'Where's your wife?' I had this sudden flash of hope that if his wife came home, she would be sure to set us free.

'She doesn't live here. We're separated and she lives with my son.'

'Oh,' I said, disappointed.

He set up the game and I started playing with him but all the time I just wanted to get off his lap and go back to Charlene. It was a boring game where a little man was climbing trees collecting things. I looked around at the papers on the floor and on the shelves beside us but couldn't really read anything. There were pages from maps, and some hand-drawn diagrams with arrows. He saw me looking at the maps and pulled a piece of paper on top of them.

'I know where you live,' he told me. 'I'd been watching you before.'

'Why?'

'Because you're so pretty.' He stroked my face again and I wriggled to try and get off his lap.

I felt creeped out by the idea he had been watching me when I didn't know he was there. I found him utterly disgusting and couldn't bear being close to him. 'I don't want to play any more,' I said.

He sounded a bit disappointed but he let me go. 'OK. Go and ask Charlene if she wants to play instead.'

I went to the sitting room door and asked her, but she shook her head. I relayed this back. 'Are you still going to take us home when it gets dark?' I asked.

'I said I would, didn't I?'

I went back to pass this news on to Charlene. 'I think we'll be home for tea tonight,' I whispered, and we grinned at each other. *Supermarket Sweep* was on the TV and we watched the contestants trying to fill their trolleys.

'I'm going to have loads of sweets later,' I said. 'Maybe we could go and get Pick 'n' Mix.'

We giggled, both cheered up by the news that we were going home. I don't know why we believed him after he'd lied to us so many times before, but we did. It made us feel happier; the thought of spending another night in that dark, smelly flat was too awful to cope with. I had a big lump in my throat, as if a stone was lodged in there and it made me want to cry all the time. I decided to try and save my tears until I was bursting in my front door at home and running up to give my dad a big hug. Until then, I had to be strong. I had to try not to break down. Surely it wouldn't be much longer.

8

Wednesday evening

Charlene

I knew Alan was playing mind games with us when he tried to sound all nice and reasonable as though he was our friend. He kept telling us how lucky we were to be with him because other men wouldn't be nearly as good to us as he was being. He kept up his line that it was our parents' fault that we were still there because they refused to pay the ransom, but I didn't believe that for a minute. He had moments when he seemed to expect us to feel sorry for him because he found it hard to cope, especially while his parents were away. I didn't buy any of this, but nevertheless, when he told us to have a bath because he was taking us home later, I was over the moon. Thank you, God, I was thinking to myself. Thank you.

He let Lisa and me go into the bathroom on our own, and I had a wee for the first time since we'd been there. I couldn't have done it with him watching. We got into the bath, chatting away in our excitement and even shrieking with laughter, until he put his head round the door and told us we'd better be quiet or the man next door might hear us. Even then we carried on chatting more quietly, speculating about what our friends would say when we got back to school, and what our parents would say and what they would have been doing while we were missing.

When we got out of the bath, he brought us our school clothes and shoes and coats and our school bags, and we got dressed and ready. He told us we had to wait until it was dark outside so we kept glancing at the window as the light gradually faded. I remember *Countdown* came on the telly and I knew it was usually on when we got home from school. We watched that, trying to think of the words along with the competitors.

We hadn't had anything to eat that day and I realised I was beginning to feel hungry. Before that my stomach had been too knotted up with fear to think about food. I wondered where he would drop us off. As long as it was somewhere in Hastings, we would be able to find our way home. Lisa knew the town back to front because she had lived there all her life.

Countdown finished and something else came on. Alan came into the room and turned the telly to another channel and sat down on the floor to watch with us. Suddenly, there was a newsflash and our pictures appeared on the screen.

'The parents of Charlene Lunnon and Lisa Hoodless, the two Hastings schoolgirls who've been missing since yesterday morning, have been making an appeal for their safe return.'

I looked at Lisa and grinned quickly. On the screen, it showed my dad and Philomena alongside Lisa's mum and dad sitting behind a long table with all these microphones in front of them. It was wonderful to see them but they all looked solemn and unhappy.

My dad did most of the talking. He said, 'Please come home, Charlene. If you're staying away because you're scared or whatever it is, there's nothing to be scared of. No one's going to get angry with you. Just come home.'

Lisa's dad spoke next and said much the same thing, asking Lisa to come back and not to worry about being in trouble.

'Look at you two,' Alan said almost proudly. 'You're all famous now with your pictures on the telly.' It was as though he thought we should be grateful to him.

Lisa and I just looked at each other. She waited for the news item to finish then asked, 'Why doesn't it say anything about us being kidnapped?'

'The police have probably told them not to mention that,' he said quickly.

'But they think we've run away,' she persisted.

'They're just saying that. It's the way these things work.'

I felt very emotional after seeing my dad's face and hearing his voice. He looked as though he hadn't slept at all and he sounded like he was on the verge of tears. I just wanted to give him a big hug. I couldn't wait to see him.

'You haven't phoned them, have you?' Lisa accused him again.

'Look, it doesn't matter if I'm taking you home anyway,' he said, and that shut us up.

When the news had finished, he went out of the room

and came back carrying the sports bag and bin liners we had been brought up to the flat in.

'Lisa, you first,' he said, beckoning for her to get inside the sports bag.

'Can't I just walk down?' she asked. 'I promise I won't run away. Why would I do that when you're letting us go anyway?'

'I can't risk anyone from round here seeing you. If you want me to let you go, you'll have to do it my way.'

Sighing, Lisa climbed into the bag and scrunched herself up small so that he could zip the top.

'I'll be back in two minutes,' he told me. 'Get the bin liners on so you're ready.'

I felt silly climbing inside the black bags but I found the place where he had made holes for my nose and eyes before and put that bit over my face. If anyone had seen me like that, it would have seemed very suspicious. I was glad I wasn't scrunched up in the sports bag though; that looked really uncomfortable.

I heard him unlocking the door and he led me out onto the landing then locked the flat behind us. No one was in sight up and down the corridor but I could hear voices somewhere and I shivered, hoping it wasn't the man next door.

'Quick! Run!' he cried, gripping my hand tightly and pulling me along to the stairs. We hurried down, round and round in circles from one landing to the next, until we reached the underground car park, then he peeled off the bin liners before he opened the boot and bundled me inside next to Lisa. He handed me a little torch so that it wouldn't be pitch black inside and I switched it on straight away.

'We're going home!' Lisa whispered to me gleefully and I gave her a quick hug.

We felt the car moving up the ramp out of the car park and turning onto the street outside, and we were both silent as he drove along. Lisa had said that Eastbourne was less than half an hour away from Hastings but it was hard to estimate the time. It seemed as though we hadn't been driving for very long when suddenly he stopped the car and came round to open the boot.

'Quick, get out!' he hissed. 'Get in the back seat.'

We were in a dark alley but I could see a road with cars passing just a little further down. It occurred to me that this was an opportunity to make a run for it, but as soon as I thought that, I dismissed the idea. He was just about to take us home anyway so what was the point? Lisa and I got in the back seat, as he instructed. He got back in and drove round the corner to a main road, and pulled up in a badly lit patch.

'I thought I should feed you before I drop you off. There's a chip shop across the road. Do you fancy some fish and chips?'

I looked at Lisa. 'Sausage and chips, please,' she said.

'What about you?' he asked me.

'The same,' I muttered.

'I'll be back in a moment,' he said. 'Don't even think about trying to get out because this is a bad neighbourhood and you would end up with someone who would be really rough with you, not like me.' Before he went, he pushed down the buttons to lock the doors.

I glanced along the street after him and I could see people passing by just ten feet away. Should we run out and ask them for help? Or would they kidnap us as well? Alan crossed the road and went into a chip shop on the other side.

Just then, Lisa noticed a newspaper on the front seat. 'Look, that's our picture!' she said. She reached over to pick it up. The headline read 'Where are they?' in great big letters and the story about us being missing took up nearly the whole of the front page. We read it excitedly.

'There are three hundred policemen looking for us and the army as well, including fifty Gurkhas!' Lisa exclaimed. 'What's a Gurkha?'

I wasn't sure but I thought it was some kind of special force like the SAS. 'That's amazing they've got so many people,' I said. I looked around. A mother was pushing a pram past the end of the alley. Lisa looked as well.

'Do you think we should just get out of here and go and ask someone for help?' she suggested.

'I don't know,' I said. 'We don't really know where we are and we might end up with someone worse than him.'

'At least he's taking us home now,' she said.

'Yeah.' There was a shadow of doubt in my head. Were we doing the right thing or should we run away, like the French girl he told us about who had thrown her bag at him and fled? Suddenly the world outside the car looked just as frightening as our predicament. I believed him when he said that it wasn't a nice neighbourhood and we could get into more trouble here. We didn't want to get out of the frying pan and into the fire, after all. We would stay here as he'd said, I decided. If we just waited patiently, we could eat our sausage and chips then he would drop us off somewhere near our house.

Lisa and I looked at each other, and I could read the same doubt in her eyes. Were we doing the right thing? We glanced across the road and saw him looking out of the chip shop towards us. If we tried to run while he was watching, he could easily catch us. We caught eyes again and hesitated. She pulled up the knob and unlocked the door, just to check whether she could, then quickly locked it again as though she was nervous that he might come back and find it unlocked. We looked at each other, both wondering the same thing. What should we do?

We hesitated too long because the next time I turned to look, he was striding back across the road towards us holding bulky packets of sausage and chips. He'd put vinegar on them and I could smell its sharpness alongside the cloying smell of chip fat as soon as he opened the door.

'Here you go, girls,' he said. 'Grub's up.'

He passed us our food and got into the front seat with his meal and we all started eating. I suddenly felt sick and lost my appetite. He noticed the newspaper on Lisa's lap. 'Did you see you're in the paper? Everyone's looking for you now,' he told us.

I chewed the corner of a chip and the grease turned my stomach. I could see that Lisa wasn't eating much of hers either.

'Come on. Don't waste good food,' he urged.

'I'm not really hungry,' Lisa said.

'Me neither,' I agreed. I was just thinking that if I got home soon I could have any food I wanted and it wouldn't be all rancid and greasy like this.

When he finished his own meal, he took our packages away from us and ate the sausages we'd left before getting out of the car and throwing the chips on top of some black plastic bin bags lying on the pavement.

He set off again and we sat back, looking out at the lights that flashed past us, blurred against the night sky.

'We're going the wrong way,' Lisa said suddenly. 'That sign was for Brighton, not Hastings.'

'It's a short cut I know,' he said.

Soon after, he turned off the well-lit main street into a narrower road that didn't have any houses on it.

'Where are we going?' Lisa asked, but he didn't answer. 'This isn't the way.'

'Damn!' he exclaimed. 'I seem to be going round in circles. I think I'm lost.'

'Just drop us off anywhere,' Lisa told him.

'Maybe it's this way,' he said, and he took a sharp left turn. Soon after that he took another left and I got a sneaking suspicion that we really were going round in circles but I didn't like to say anything to Lisa.

'We're definitely lost,' he said again. 'That was a wrong turn.'

'Please can we get out now?' Lisa pleaded, but he ignored her.

A little knot of panic was tightening inside me. I didn't care where he let us out, I just wanted it to be soon.

I could feel fear growing inside me. What was I doing in this strange man's car in the darkness, looking out at a place I didn't know, far from my home and my family? I'd been away for two days now; another night was coming. What was Alan planning to do with us? I was sure now that he wasn't taking us home.

It was totally black outside and we couldn't see any streetlamps at all. I was angry and frustrated with myself. Why hadn't we jumped out of the car at the chip shop? Why had I trusted him when he'd lied to us at every turn so far?

My fear level rose even higher as he turned off the road and I realised he was driving on grass. Were we going across a field?

'I need a wee,' Lisa said. 'Stop the car. I need to get out.'

I wasn't sure if she was trying to think of an excuse to get away or if she really needed a wee, but he pulled up and opened the back door to let her get out of the car.

'There's a bush right there,' he said. 'Go and have your wee.' He looked at me. 'Why don't you get out and stretch your legs?' he suggested.

I got out of the car because I didn't want to be left on my own with him, and that's when I realised that the sea was right in front of us. There was mushy grass underfoot and a cliff edge and then sea stretching right out to the horizon.

'Where are we?' I asked, looking round for Lisa. My voice was very shaky.

'Come and look,' he said, grabbing my jumper and

pulling me over towards the cliff edge. It was very windy that night and I could hear the waves crashing hard onto the stones below. I couldn't see very well but I knew we were right on the edge of the cliff and I was petrified. What if a gust of wind blew us over? We were too close to the edge but he was standing right behind me so I couldn't back away.

Suddenly he gave me a sharp push and I lost my footing. Stones slid away under my feet and clattered over the edge into thin air, and I would have fallen after them if he hadn't been hanging on tightly to my jumper. He yanked me back again and I sank down onto the grass, my heart beating harder than it had ever done in my life before.

I was panting heavily and my chest felt tight as though I was going to have an asthma attack. I wished I had an inhaler with me. I was gasping for every breath. The whole incident had only taken about five seconds but I knew he could easily have let go and I would be dead now. Did he plan to kill us? Was that what he was going to do next?

As if reading my mind, he told me quietly, 'No, I think I'm going to keep you for one more day.'

I couldn't speak. The breath had been knocked right out of me. I've never been as scared as I was sitting there in the blackness with a huge drop down to the sea right in front of me. I crawled further up the grass, trying to get out of danger, scared that the cliff edge could crumble beneath me.

The man was pacing around muttering to himself. I

heard him say something to Lisa and she came running over. 'Are you alright?'

'He's going to kill us,' I gasped, finding it hard to speak. 'He just nearly killed me!'

'Oh my God!' she breathed, crouching down and clutching my shoulder. 'Did he say that?'

'Back in the car, girls,' he commanded, and his tone was harsh again now, not friendly as it had been at the chip shop. 'No more talking.'

He opened the boot, grabbed hold of us and pushed Lisa and then me inside before slamming the lid. The thought occurred to me that he might just roll the whole car off the cliff. Was that his plan? I could hardly breathe as I waited to see what would happen next, and my chest felt as though it had a tight band strapped all around it. There was a loud drumming sound in my ears and my cheeks were burning.

'What's he doing?' Lisa whispered and I could hear the terror in her voice.

For a while, nothing happened. He was just sitting in the driver's seat, as if trying to make a decision.

'Please, God, help us,' I whispered back, and we clung to each other. Her fingers were digging into my arm.

The car started and we felt it begin to move. I held my breath, waiting to see if the ground would disappear beneath us and we would be hurtling off the cliff edge into the sea below. The tyres rolled over grass and then I felt a bump and could sense from the vibrations that we were driving on the road again. I breathed out with a big sigh.

There was no doubt in my mind that he had almost killed me out there on the cliff edge. He'd been thinking about it and had changed his mind at the last minute. But he'd said he only wanted us for another day. I supposed that meant he would kill us after that. Unless some miracle happened before then, I only had twenty-four hours left to live.

Lisa

It was on that cliff edge that everything changed. I realised in a flash that he had lied to us about letting us go. He had no intention of taking us home because no matter how much we promised him otherwise, he knew we would go to the police. He wasn't going to set us free.

I didn't see him nearly pushing Charlene over the edge but when I had finished having a wee, I came out from behind a bush and he grabbed me and hustled me over to a spot where I could see the sea stretching to the horizon right in front of me. Two more steps and we would both have gone over. It felt very high up and I was terrified.

'Where's Charlene?' I asked, scared that he might have pushed her already.

'She's over there,' he said, and shoved me in the direction of where she sat panting on the ground.

When I crouched down beside her, she whispered, 'He's going to kill us. He just nearly killed me,' and my heart leapt into my mouth.

I looked around to see if I could see any lights at all. If

a car had driven past, I would have rushed out in front of it and flagged it down. If only I could see a house somewhere, or a person walking a dog – but there was nothing. Just the sound of the wind gusting past and the waves crashing onto the shore below and a black sky above.

Where on earth were we? We were obviously on a very high cliff edge, but there were quite a few of these around Eastbourne. I didn't recognise the place in the dark.

He walked up and down for a while then he hustled us back into the boot of the car and we hugged each other tightly. What was he going to do now? Was he going to take us somewhere else to kill us?

I'd never known anyone who had died. My nan is quite religious and she always told me that when you die you go to heaven and meet up with all your friends and family members up there when they die as well, so death sounded quite nice in a way. But I knew absolutely that I didn't want to die. I would still rather go home and get beaten up by my brother and have my clothes stolen by my sister and do science lessons at school – anything, really, just as long as I could live.

But now I knew our kidnapper for what he really was: a liar, who wasn't going to take us home ever. He'd never spoken to our parents, I was sure about that, and he didn't want a ransom for us. He was a horrible, pathetic man, who one minute was begging us to be his friends and trying to make us feel sorry for him, and the next ordering us about and threatening us. He wanted to rape us and when he got fed up with that, he'd probably kill us.

We both lay in the back of the car in shock. Charlene

was breathing in funny little gasps. Our dreams of going home were shattered. We had let ourselves truly believe that we were on our way back to our families, and were happily looking forward to bursting in the front door of our houses and shouting 'Hello! I'm back!' Now we had to face the fact that we were with a madman who wasn't going to let us go. It was a huge blow, and we just lay in that boot trembling and hugging each other, neither of us able to speak.

We weren't driving for long this time – maybe ten or fifteen minutes – when we felt him pull the car off the road. When he opened the boot, I saw that we were in the garage at his parents' house again. We didn't want to let go of each other but he grabbed my arm and pulled me up.

'Stay there!' he told Charlene as he pushed me into the sports bag.

'What are you going to do with us?' I asked, but he didn't answer me. His mood had changed and he seemed unpredictable and dangerous. He zipped up the top of the bag and carried me out of the garage and into the house.

Once we were inside he took me into a sitting room at the front of the house. He let me climb out of the bag and sit on the sofa, then he put the television on.

'Don't move a muscle,' he said. 'I'll be back in a moment.'

I looked around the room. Like the other room I'd been in at the back of the house, it was obviously an old person's room, with old-fashioned ornaments and pictures, and dark brownish-coloured furniture and a swirly-patterned carpet. I heard him come back into the house and Charlene was with him because he said 'this way' as he led her down the corridor. They seemed to be going into the room I'd been in before. I realised it was only yesterday we'd been there but so much had happened since then that it seemed like a lifetime ago.

I huddled up to the back of the sofa, shaking and terrified. I didn't even consider trying to look out the window or search for a telephone. All I could think about was the method he might use to kill us. Would he get a knife and stab us? Or maybe strangle us with his bare hands? Or did he plan to take us back to that cliff and push us over? Whatever he did, I hoped it would be quick and that it wouldn't hurt too much. Was he planning to kill us now, in this house? Charlene had said he was going to keep us for another day but it was clear that we couldn't trust him. He had lied and lied and lied to us right from the word go.

The film on television was about two old women who were sisters, and one of them was so jealous of the other that she went crazy and tied her sister to a kind of platform with her legs and arms pulled wide in a star shape. Then she got a chainsaw and set it running so the jagged blade was going round and round and she began cutting up through the wood between her sister's legs. Her sister screamed and screamed in agony as the blade cut her in two and there was blood spraying everywhere, but the jealous one kept laughing with a hideous cackle. I couldn't stop watching but my head was pounding and my mouth was dry. Afterwards, the jealous sister buried the cut-up body in the snow outside. It was just horrible. I'd never seen a film like that before and couldn't believe anyone would want to watch such things. It was doubly horrible for me as I sat there wondering how Alan was going to murder us. For the first time in my life, I realised that night how much true evil there is in the world.

Suddenly I heard Charlene screaming, and it was definitely a scream of pain. I only hesitated for a split-second before I jumped off the sofa and ran down the hall to the back room.

When I threw the door open, I didn't understand what I was seeing at first. Charlene was naked and kneeling on all fours on the floor. Alan still had his shirt on but he'd pulled down his trousers and he was ramming his willy at her from behind. She turned round to look at me, and the expression on her face was so appalled and embarrassed that I backed away towards the door and looked the other way.

'What are you doing?' I shouted at him. 'You promised you wouldn't do that any more. You broke your promise and you're a liar and I hate you!' I just kept shouting at him until he stood up and came towards me.

'Be quiet,' he ordered. 'You'll waken the neighbours and they're bad people. They would do awful things to you.'

'You're a bad person and you're doing awful things to us,' I accused him. 'Just stop it and let us go. You said you would. You promised.'

I felt like crying but I managed to stop myself by

focusing on my anger. He looked at me for a minute then he looked back at Charlene, still on her knees there and peering down at the floor.

'Alright, we'd better go then,' he said. 'Get dressed,' he ordered Charlene. 'And you' – he looked at me – 'get in the bag.'

I thought about refusing but any courage I'd been feeling a minute ago had completely evaporated. I'd had my victory making him stop trying to rape Charlene and I knew I wasn't going to get any more. He took a step towards me and the look in his eyes was cold and cruel. I thought he was going to hit me so I turned and ran back to the front room and stepped into the bag again. He followed me in and zipped up the top, then went back to say something I couldn't hear to Charlene before he carried me outside to the car.

Had I made him mad? Would he take us back to the cliff again and push us over? I decided that if he let us out of the car on the cliff top I would just run off into the dark as fast as I could. I'd tell Charlene to do the same at the next opportunity we got. We should have done it when we were sitting outside the chip shop. How trusting we had been, thinking he would just buy us dinner and take us back home! We wouldn't fall for his tricks any more. He wasn't someone we could trust, he was a criminal who had been in jail and who had kidnapped other children as well as us.

He brought Charlene out to the car and she wouldn't meet my eye as she climbed in. I waited until he started the engine and began to reverse out, then I whispered to her: 'The next time we get a chance, we have to make a run for it. Both of us. If we go in different directions, he won't be able to catch us both and we should just keep running until we find someone who can get help. OK?'

'OK,' she said quietly.

'Even if he takes us back to the cliff edge and it's really dark, just run away in the other direction from the sea and you'll come to a house or a hotel before long.'

'Alright.'

I found her hand and squeezed it. I heard her sniff and wondered if she was crying but didn't like to ask. Charlene hardly ever cried. I was the crier of the two of us, so that made it even more sad when she did cry.

We lay in silence for the rest of the journey. I was planning what I would say if I ran away and knocked on someone's door. There wouldn't be time for a long explanation. I decided I would just say, 'I'm one of the missing girls. Please call the police!' I rehearsed it in my head and thought that would work. It sounded urgent enough.

Soon we felt the car take a right turn and head downhill, and I was pretty sure I knew where we were. It sounded like the underground car park again. Would there be a chance to run when he opened the boot?

But there wasn't. He just grabbed my sleeve and pulled me out first then slammed down the lid on Charlene. I wriggled to try to loosen his grip but he grasped me firmly and pushed me down into the sports bag before carrying me up the stairs to his flat. He took me into the sitting room and let me out, then told me sternly not to move until he brought Charlene upstairs.

I heard him locking the door behind him, but as soon as I judged he had gone, I got up and went out to the hall to check. That's when I noticed that the door handle had been removed from the inside. There was nothing I could hold onto to try and pull the door open. I slipped my fingers into the hole where it should have been and yanked it with all my strength but it was firmly locked. I ran through to the sitting-room window. I couldn't see anyone on the street outside and there were no cars going past. It felt like the early hours of the morning but it must have late evening. I ran into the bedroom to try and check the window there but then I reckoned that I didn't have any time left before he arrived back at the flat, so I had no choice but to go back and sit quietly on the sofa.

When he came in with Charlene, he said, 'It's late, girls. Why don't you sleep on the bed tonight?' He pointed at the single bed in the corner. 'You'll be comfier there. I've got to go and pick up my parents from the airport in a while but I'll be back before you wake up. If you're thinking of trying to escape, just remember about the man next door and what he would do to you. OK?'

He picked up the quilt and arranged it on the bed, then put a cushion at either end for us to use as pillows. He beckoned us over and we just obeyed. First of all he made us strip off our school clothes and put on those big white t-shirts again then we climbed into the bed in a top-to-tail position.

'Sleep tight, don't let the bedbugs bite,' he said before he left the room and switched the light off.

Neither of us spoke. We were shattered from the events of the past few hours and I know that I fell asleep really quickly. My brain had had enough and couldn't cope with any more. I needed the blankness of sleep.

9
Thursday morning

Charlene

When I woke up on the Thursday morning, all was quiet in the flat. Lisa was still sound asleep and I didn't like to disturb her. The events of the previous evening came rushing back and all my muscles tensed rigid with fear. He had almost killed me on that cliff top and then said he wanted me for just one more day, so it sounded as though today was going to be the day I died. This was it. My last day on earth.

When would he do it? As soon as he got up? Or would he want to rape us again first? I decided he would probably wait till after dark so that no one saw him. That gave us a few more hours to live – and it gave him a few more hours to do those disgusting things to us. Although Lisa had also been in the bedroom with him now, I was still getting the brunt of it. It was just my bad luck that I was so much bigger.

My cheeks burned when I remembered Lisa walking in on us at his mum and dad's house. I'd felt ashamed for her to see me like that, as though I was doing something wrong. Would Lisa have thought that I was going along with it and letting him do those things instead of fighting back? I didn't want to do them, but I was so petrified when I was on my own with him that I did whatever he wanted me to. The panic when he put his hand over my mouth and nose was so intense that I was sure I was going to suffocate or have an asthma attack. I let him move me into all the different positions he wanted and I just closed my eyes and gritted my teeth. The pain had been worse than ever and it had felt different, deeper. I was pretty sure he had succeeded in getting inside me and that made me feel sick to my stomach. I knew in my heart of hearts that I was only doing what I had to do to survive but it was humiliating that Lisa had seen me like that. I remembered the shock and disbelief on her face and blushed even deeper.

We had been so stupid and naive all along. If only I had run away back in Cornfield Terrace and hammered on doors until someone came out to help. Even if he had driven off with Lisa in the boot I could have memorised his car number plate and then the police would have found him quickly. Or we could both have run away while he was in the chip shop. It seemed crazy now that we hadn't done that. I could even have started screaming and tried to run away in the underground car park or at his mum and dad's house, if I had dared. All the time I'd just believed that if we behaved ourselves and co-operated that he would take us home when he'd finished with us. We gave him the benefit of the doubt and it looked as though that would be our downfall.

There was a great big lump in my throat and I wanted to cry but the tears wouldn't come. I've never been one for crying. There have been so many bad things in my life right from the start that I just decided I had to get on with it and not make a fuss every single time. There were the days when I was taken away from Mum as a little kid and put into all those foster homes; the times when my hopes of going back to her were raised and then dashed; the friends I left behind with each change of foster parents; and then all the mind games that Bert played on me, making me feel as though I was dirty and worthless. If I'd cried about all that, I'd have had no tears left.

The only time I cried a lot was the year after Mum died. My head was full of memories of the good times I'd had with her when we were two girls together, just having fun and cuddles, and it felt unbearable that we would never do that again. When she was clean of drink and drugs, I thought she was the best mum in the world. In the mornings we used to cuddle up on the sofa and watch *The Big Breakfast* on TV together. If it was winter, she'd bring through the quilt from her bed to wrap around us. Every time the story on the news changed, they used to change the background colour behind the presenter's head and Mum and I would sit there guessing what the next colour would be: 'Orange!' 'Green!' 'Pink!' 'Blue!' If I got it right, she'd give me a prize of a chocolate from the bowl on the coffee table.

There was a grocer's shop just across the road where you could buy things by the scoop instead of having to get a whole boxful. We'd go over there and buy a couple of scoops of cornflakes and a scoop of banana milkshake powder, then we'd go home and have milkshakes with our cereal. That was a real treat.

She'd chat to me as if I was her best friend rather than her small daughter. She'd discuss her boyfriends with me, or tell me where she'd been the night before and who was there, and she'd paint my nails in pretty shades of pink and give me a spray of perfume. I just loved our girly moments.

Even in the evenings when she was drunk or stoned, if she didn't have a boyfriend there, she'd let me cuddle up on the sofa and watch grown-up films with her. I never wanted to stay in my bed so I'd come creeping out asking if I could stay up a bit longer and she'd grin and say 'Alright then'. She always told me I was her favourite of all her children, and her best friend in the world.

Mum had five kids altogether – Carol who was about twenty when I was born, Alan who was about sixteen, Rose who was about ten and another brother whose name I don't know, who I've never met. None of them lived with us when I was growing up, because Mum was actually in prison for shoplifting when she found out she was pregnant with me. That makes her sound like a bad person, but in fact she just had an illness that she couldn't recover from and that finally killed her: the illness of addiction.

She and my dad were only together for a couple of months. It was a relationship based solely on drugs and they hated each other afterwards to the extent that they couldn't be in the same room as each other. I never like to talk to Dad about my mum because he has such a low opinion of her, but to me she was the only mum I knew and I cherish all the good memories I have.

Auntie Vera was lovely to me the whole time I stayed in their house, like a surrogate mother in many ways. In the last year I was at hers, when my emotions about Mum dying finally spilled out, I tried to hide it from Dad because I knew how much he hated her – but I think he knew anyway. That Christmas of 1997, I really wanted a doll called Baby Lulu that I'd seen on the telly. If you bounced her on your knee, she laughed and cried and even breathed – but she cost sixty whole pounds.

Auntie Vera sat me down and told me that it was the most popular toy that Christmas and she was really sorry but it had sold out so they wouldn't be able to get me one. Dad arrived on Christmas Eve to stay for the holidays and he said, 'I've got you a present but I'm afraid I couldn't get you that doll you wanted. Sorry!' But when I woke up on Christmas morning Dad handed me a big box and I ripped the paper off and there was Baby Lulu inside! I think he'd had to trek round every single toyshop in London looking for it. It was my best Christmas ever.

I hadn't played with Baby Lulu for a while now. She was still sitting in my room along with all my teddies, but I had cut her hair short and given her a few hand-drawn tattoos and made some crazy clothes for her, so she looked quite different than she had when she came out of the box. I thought about my bedroom at home and all my toys waiting there. Who would get them if I were killed? What would Dad do with them?

Another thought occurred to me. What if Alan didn't kill us but just kept us there as his prisoners to have sex with? After a while everyone would think we were dead and they would stop looking for us and we'd be stuck in that disgusting flat for ever, day after day, doing what he wanted us to do. Was this what my life was going to be like from now on?

I suddenly realised I hadn't heard him moving around that morning, then remembered that he said he was picking his parents up from the airport. Could he have gone away and left us on our own? Or was he back already and sleeping next door? I didn't dare get up to go and check. Lisa stirred slightly and I hissed her name.

'Whadisit?' she murmured, and I could see there was a moment when she woke up before she remembered where we were. She was just thinking she was having a sleepover at mine or something until the terrible truth came back to her. She lifted her head and looked around the dingy, depressing room. 'Where is he?'

'I don't know if he's here. I can't hear him.'

'I've got to go for a wee so I'll find out.'

She slipped out of bed then tiptoed out the door into the hall. I waited for a few seconds then I heard the loo being flushed and Lisa's head appeared.

'He's not here. The bedroom door is open a crack and I can't see him.'

I got up and pulled the t-shirt down to my knees. 'Shall we have a look around in case we can find anything to help us escape?'

The first thing I did was to check the front door but it

was firmly locked and the handle was missing on the inside. There was no way we could have opened it. Then I peeped into his bedroom and had a look at the clock: it was just before eight o'clock. I didn't stay in there for long though because that room gave me the shudders. Next I decided to look in the office because he seemed to have lots of papers in there, and I also thought that if there was a phone in the house, surely it would be in there. Lisa came with me and we started sifting through all the bits of paper that covered every surface.

The first thing I noticed was that there were lots of pictures of children that looked as though they had been torn out of magazines. Then Lisa showed me the maps she had seen the day before and we noticed that he had marked on them where the schools were in each area – it was creepy to look at it. And then I caught my breath as I came across something that seemed to be about torture. I couldn't read very well so I handed it to Lisa.

'It's a list of children and things that were done to them. Oh, it's disgusting!' she cried and dropped it on the floor.

'Do you think he tortured them?'

'I don't know.'

We looked at each other. 'Maybe we should try to leave this place the way it was so he doesn't know we've been in here?' I suggested. So far he had been very calm and quiet when he spoke to us and I didn't want to see what he would be like if he got angry.

We tidied up as best we could then crept back into the sitting room and climbed into bed.

'Do you think he's had lots of other children here before us?' Lisa asked.

I shrugged. If he had, where were they? What had happened to them? They must be dead because if they were still alive they would have told the police and he would be locked up in jail.

'What if he doesn't come back?' Lisa continued. 'He might just leave us locked in here until we die of starvation.'

'If he's not back by the time it starts to get dark, we have to try and escape,' I said. 'Maybe we could tie sheets together and hang them out of the window and climb down to the roof below, then we could shout out until someone saw us.'

We looked up at the window trying to imagine this but it was tiny – only about the size of a picture frame – and quite high up. There was nowhere to tie a sheet onto and it was just too far to fall on the other side.

'Or we could lean out the window and start shouting really loudly,' Lisa suggested.

'What about the man next door?' Neither of us was willing to take the risk of falling into another man's hands. Even though he'd lied to us, we believed Alan when he said his neighbour was worse than him. After all, Alan had showed us that bad men who wanted to hurt little girls really did exist. Why shouldn't there be another one living in the same squalid way as Alan himself? I shuddered to think what 'worse' might be like.

'You never know – he might take us home today?' Lisa suggested in a quiet voice.

I didn't want to say anything to upset her but I didn't believe that any more. He had no intention of letting us go. Either we escaped or he would kill us: that's all I believed now. I felt so depressed that it was too much effort to speak. I wriggled down under the covers and turned my face to the wall.

We were glad we'd got back into bed when we did because soon afterwards we heard the key in the lock and Alan came back into the flat. He locked the door behind him and we both pretended to be asleep when he looked into the sitting room. He went into the office and we heard some things being moved around. We could hear him muttering to himself and he seemed a bit agitated. My stomach twisted into a tight knot, wondering what he was going to do with us next.

Next time he came into the sitting room, he pushed the door open with a clatter and said 'Time to get up, girls!' as he walked over and pulled back the curtains. Grey January light flooded in. 'Let's see what they're saying about you on the news this morning.'

He switched on the television and crouched on the floor in front of it. Lisa and I got up and walked over to the sofa so we could see the screen, desperate to find out what was going on. What were our parents doing? Were the police still looking for us up in London?

There were lots of other news stories first but then it came round to nine o'clock and we were the headline news. They were still using the same photos, but the words they were saying filled me with horror. 'Hopes are fading of finding the missing girls alive after forty-eight hours have passed since they disappeared on their way to school. There have been no new sightings since the initial reports that they had been seen in London and detectives say that their leads are drying up.'

I stared at the screen open-mouthed. It had only been two days since we were kidnapped. How could they give up after two days?

Then my dad's face came on the screen. His skin was as white as a sheet and his eyes had a horrible haunted look. When he spoke, he stumbled a bit over the words. 'I hope she is somewhere safe and warm,' he said. 'If some misguided person is looking after her, all I have to say to you is please send her home.' His voice cracked at the end of the sentence.

I looked at Alan to see if he was listening but he didn't seem to care. Then I looked back at my dad's face and I realised something awful. He thought I was dead already. I could tell from his expression. He'd given up hope. I covered my face with my hands and felt cold all over. My skin tightened and I started to shiver.

For me, it was the lowest point yet.

The newsreader moved on to the next story and Alan looked round at us with a strange expression. 'They're not even looking for you any more,' he said. 'They don't even care about you.'

'They do so!' Lisa cried. 'You wait and see.'

I didn't say anything. I just couldn't get the image of my dad's face out of my head. He looked old and tired and heartbroken. He looked as though his whole world had fallen apart.

Lisa

Charlene was really upset after seeing her dad doing an appeal on the telly. As soon as Alan left the room, she whispered to me, 'He thinks I'm dead.'

Deep down I had to agree with her that his face looked grief-stricken, but I tried to reassure her. 'He wouldn't be making an appeal like that if he'd given up hope. He's still trying to find us. That's why he did it.'

I wondered why my mum and dad hadn't done this appeal with him. Maybe they really had given up hope. Keith seemed to think we were staying with someone, and I could see why he would think that because it was January. The nights were freezing so we would never have survived the cold if we were sleeping outside. Did they still think we had run away? Who on earth had started that rumour? None of my close friends would have said anything so stupid.

The police had obviously gone to school and asked if anyone had any idea where we might have gone. I guessed that someone who didn't know Charlene and me very well but who wanted to feel important must have come forward and made up that story about Charlene's mum's grave. It was such a stupid thing to do because it had made the police look for us in London instead of closer to home. No one would ever find us here in a block of flats in the middle of Eastbourne. Since we'd been there, we hadn't heard another soul in the building – not even a postman delivering mail in the morning. It seemed completely deserted.

It was a horrible and depressing flat, with its small boxy rooms leading off a long gloomy corridor, the lack of windows and the pervading smell of cabbagey damp. Everywhere was grimy with deeply ingrained dirt, as though it hadn't been cleaned for years. Probably some of the dirt came from the people who lived there before Alan. I tried not to touch the walls and I always rinsed out the glass thoroughly before I had a glass of water. The kitchen surfaces felt sticky with grease and the bath was stained yellow, while fungus was growing on the ceiling up above it.

Alan was grimy as well. His fingers were brown with nicotine, his teeth were a brownish-yellow, and although he had bathed twice since we'd been there, he still had a nasty smell about him, the aroma of stale tobacco and stale sweat mixed together. I loved to be clean and I hated mess and dirt, so I found it particularly disgusting to breathe in the air around him.

Charlene and I sat on the sofa, dressed only in our over-sized white t-shirts, and watched the *Trisha* show that morning. There was a story about a man who had been having an affair behind his wife's back and she was trying to decide whether to forgive him or not. The audience were booing and hissing at him and not really giving him a chance to speak. I knew my mum watched that show and I wondered if she was watching it that morning. Was this really how she spent her time while we were at school? I supposed that with a young baby, she had to be around the house a lot because the baby needed naps, but I didn't know how she could stand to watch shows like that. I might be only ten, but I could see how dumb the people were. Surely if you had a problem in your marriage, going on a TV show was one of the worst possible ways of trying to fix it?

Alan was bustling around that morning. He seemed to be worried about something because he was pacing from room to room and muttering under his breath. On previous mornings he had sat down to chat to us and tried to be friendly but there was obviously something on his mind that day. Was it because his parents were back from their trip now? Or was it something on the television that we hadn't noticed? Charlene and I were very wary whenever he came into the room. We didn't move from the sofa or ask him any questions – instead we tried to keep quiet and not come to his attention. I had the distinct impression that he might be close to cracking and that frightened me. Was he building up the courage to kill us later? Was he trying to decide how to do it?

He popped his head round the door. 'Lisa, could you come with me?' he asked.

I don't know where I got the courage from but I said, 'No, I don't want to.'

'I just need to talk to you. It's important.'

I shook my head and stared at my lap.

'Come on, Lisa. Don't keep me waiting.'

'You can talk to me here,' I said. 'I don't want to come to the bedroom with you.'

He glared at me for a minute, as if trying to decide whether to drag me through anyway, then he gave a sigh of exasperation and stomped off down the hall. I made a face at Charlene – a mixture of amazement that I'd refused him like that, and fear about what would happen next. We didn't talk about it, though. We just sat in silence, not wanting to give Alan an excuse to come back into the room and tell us off. He seemed very unpredictable and unapproachable that morning.

Trisha finished and then it was *This Morning.* I was watching it but without seeing anything because my mind was buzzing with worrying about our situation and what we were going to do.

I wondered if my dad would make another appeal, as Keith had. He would hate being the centre of attention in a room with lots of people pointing cameras at him. My dad was a very private person who didn't want anyone else knowing his business. He was a real homebody, just going out to do his work during the day and staying at home in the evenings. Mum was the one who liked going out to clubs and pubs with her friends and Dad would babysit for us. At weekends, he stayed at home and worked in the garden. He didn't have many friends; I couldn't think of anyone who visited him. All the visitors to the house were for Mum.

But when he was in a good mood, there was a quietly wacky side to my dad. He was very tall and lanky and sometimes he would make us laugh by swinging between the kitchen units, resting his weight on his arms and looking like an orang-utan. He was so gangly that it always made me giggle.

I knew I was Dad's favourite. Both James and Christine got into trouble at school and played up at home and I was the good little girl of the family who had never caused him any worry – until now.

I wished with all my heart that I were back at home, sitting on the big white furry rug in front of the fire while Dad sat in his armchair and we all watched a video together. It was my favourite place to snuggle up in the evening. Dad would tell me off for hogging all the heat, but in a jokey kind of a way that I knew he didn't mean. We'd have lots of snacks laid out – sweets and crisps and juice – to munch during the film. It was just cosy and normal.

Suddenly the door burst open and Alan came in. 'Charlene, come with me,' he ordered, in a voice that didn't allow for any arguments.

She looked round at me.

'Now!' he said. 'Come on, I haven't got all day.' He took a step towards her as if he was going to pull her up and drag her through to the bedroom.

She stood up slowly and glanced round at me one more time. I gave her a sympathetic look but what could I do? Maybe he just wanted to talk, as he'd said to me. I tried to convince myself of this as she followed him down the corridor, her feet dragging.

I sat on the sofa, overcome with guilt that once again he was taking her and not me. It was so unfair. Of course, part of me was very relieved and that made the guilt worse. I had so many emotions all mixed up together that I couldn't think straight. I strained my ears to listen for any noise from the bedroom but I couldn't hear anything over the sound of the television.

I felt utterly miserable sitting there, as though I had let Charlene down somehow. It was curious because on the outside, she was always the more confident of the two of us, the one who was the leader and made the decisions about what we were going to do next, but in the flat here she seemed subdued and defeated. It was hardly surprising that she was terrified after he dangled her over the cliff edge like that. She was probably still in shock.

After a while, I got up and tiptoed through to the kitchen to get a glass of water. There was silence in the bedroom as I passed the door and I hoped that was a good sign. I hoped that meant he was just looking at her or something, but not raping her.

They were gone for a long time. *This Morning* finished and there was a talk show with people I didn't recognise. I got up and pressed the button on the set to flick through the channels, because there was no remote control. On one channel they were showing Keith's appeal again so I watched it once more. He stumbled over his words, looking very pale, as if he hadn't slept. I got the impression someone had told him what to say instead of letting him talk in his own words. I could see why Charlene thought it looked as though he had given up hope, but I reasoned that the police must still be looking for us. You don't give up after two days. I was sure I could remember seeing appeals on the telly for people who had been missing for a week or more.

I sat down and watched the rest of the news programme without really seeing it. All the time I was racking my brains, trying to come up with a solution to our problem. If Granddad were there, what would he advise me to do? Or what would Mr Okrainetz say? I tried to picture all the cleverest people I knew and imagine what they might suggest but nothing new came to me. We needed a plan. I got up and had another look out of the tiny window but I couldn't see how I would open it and, even if I could, there was no way down. It was just too far to the shop roof. Could anyone see me from down below on the street? I could make out a few figures a long way off but none of them looked up. I stood at the window for ages and didn't hear Charlene and Alan emerging from the bedroom and coming down the hall.

'What are you doing?' he snapped at me. 'Come away from the window.'

Charlene crept over to the sofa and sat down carefully. I walked over and sat down beside her.

'It's your turn now,' Alan told me firmly. 'Come on.'

I looked at Charlene and she wouldn't meet my eye.

'Come on, Lisa. Now.' He stood waiting by the door. I considered saying no again, as I had done before, but the expression on his face didn't look as though he was willing to back down. It wouldn't be fair for me to say no because maybe he'd take Charlene back in again instead of me.

Feeling sick to my stomach, I stood up and walked across to him, then down the corridor to his dark little prison cell of a bedroom.

10

Thursday afternoon

Charlene

Lisa refused when Alan tried to take her to the bedroom, but then he came back for me instead and he wasn't going to take no for an answer. He was behaving in a scary way so I didn't dare make a fuss. He was sort of distant and obviously had a lot on his mind. When he had sex with me he didn't try to talk to me nicely or anything any more. It was as if he was a robot just doing the same things time and time again. He'd stop and play with himself for a bit to get hard, then he'd turn me into a different position and it would start all over again. After a while I was so sore and swollen that he couldn't do much. He had some kind of cream that he said would reduce the swelling and he rubbed that in, then he just lay touching me all over and trying to make me touch him.

I became completely numb. I disappeared inside my own thoughts and didn't talk to him at all or react to anything he was doing. As far as I could, I completely ignored him. It got so monotonous that I wondered how he could keep going without getting bored to tears but he had a kind of nervous energy about him that day. He seemed wired. I worried that he was doing as much as he could because he felt that time was running out, as though we wouldn't be around for much longer.

All that day, he took us into his bedroom in turns. I never had a chance to talk to Lisa because as soon as he had finished with me, he took her in and as soon as he finished with her, he wanted me back in there again. While Lisa was in with him, I flicked through the TV channels looking for news broadcasts because I wanted to see the film of my dad again. There were only the five channels – no Sky or anything – but I found a newsflash mid-afternoon. It was just a short broadcast, and it showed Dad saying 'Please let my little girl come home.' It was so sweet that I had tears in my eyes. It was comforting to know that he was out there looking for me, doing everything he could possibly think of. It made me feel very loved, even though I was upset about his exhausted appearance and the desperation in his eyes.

Poor old Dad. As if he hadn't had a hard enough life already! I was so proud of the way he had managed to get himself off drugs. He'd been using heroin for about twenty years and had tried to stop loads of times before without success but the programme at Phoenix House had finally helped him to beat his addiction. I must have been about seven or eight when he took me to visit it. He had been resident there for a while, and then he found a flat in nearby Bexhill so he could carry on attending their support groups. He once explained to me that the difference between Phoenix House and other clinics he had tried was that they made you take responsibility for yourself. No one came round telling you what to do. They just put the choices in front of you and you had to take them.

The day I visited there with him, everyone made a huge fuss of me and I could tell he was very popular. Someone went off to the kitchen and got me some chocolate ice cream, which was one of my favourite things. They all seemed like lovely people.

Dad also used to take me to the beach at Camber Sands. He spoiled me rotten on our days out, and he spoiled me even more once I came to live with him. Whatever I wanted, I got. My hamster, new clothes, friends to stay over – he couldn't deny me anything I asked for. I'd had a tough time in the early years of my life but at the age of ten, I thought it was all going to work at last. That was, until Alan came along.

It must have been late afternoon because the children's programmes had come on the telly when he emerged from the bedroom with Lisa and asked us if we wanted something to eat. We both said, 'Yes, please.' I wasn't especially hungry, despite the fact that we hadn't eaten anything that day. We'd had our packed lunches on the first day and a few mouthfuls of chips the night before. It wasn't much but I still didn't have an appetite. We asked for food only because at least if he was getting food for us we would get a break from the constant trips to the bedroom.

'What do you want?' he asked.

Lisa asked for pizza and chips and I didn't say anything.

'OK, I'll just go to the shop downstairs. You two be good while I'm away. I won't be long.'

We listened to him locking the door behind him, then Lisa turned to me. 'Are you OK?'

'Yeah,' I shrugged. 'You?'

Tears came to her eyes but she blinked them back. 'Yeah. What are we going to do though?'

I shook my head. I had completely run out of ideas. Could we rush out when he opened the front door and try to run past him onto the stairs? But then the man next door might get us and we couldn't face the thought of that. Should we take our chances jumping out of the window? But we couldn't even work out how to open it. There was nothing in the flat that we could use to attack him: no knives, no guns, no objects we could hit him over the head with. The only thing we agreed was that if he took us out of the flat again, say to the cliff top, then we would make a run for it.

We watched telly for a while then Lisa asked, 'What do you miss most about your old life?'

I'd been thinking about that in some detail already, and immediately came out with a list: 'My dad; my hamster; sleeping in my own bed; chicken nuggets and chips; and my favourite TV programmes.'

'I miss my granddad, my school friends and my own bed,' she said. 'And freedom. Being able to do what you want without that creep dragging you off the whole time.'

'What do you *not* miss?' I asked.

'Being beaten up by my brother,' she answered, which was fair enough. 'And I hate sharing a bedroom with my sister.'

I knew she hated sharing with her sister. Things had got so bad they had a line across the middle of the floor and neither of them was supposed to cross into the other's side.

'I don't miss PE,' I told her. 'The worst thing is when we're doing rounders. I can't run very fast because of my asthma and everyone is watching me. The whole team is shouting at me to go faster so they can get to the next base themselves and I just can't do it so I always let everyone down.'

'At least when we get to secondary school we won't have to do rounders any more,' she told me.

I looked at her. Would we ever go to secondary school, or was Alan planning to kill us tonight? She seemed more optimistic about our situation than me but I decided not to contradict her.

'We're going to be friends for life now, aren't we?' she asked.

'Definitely,' I said. 'For ever and ever.'

The key turned in the lock and we heard Alan coming back in. 'Pizza and chips coming up,' he shouted from the hall.

I tried to decide if I felt hungry or not. I thought back to the Haribos I'd been munching just before Alan kidnapped us and wished I had some sweets in the flat. That's what I felt like – something sweet and easy to eat, rather than stodgy pizza and chips.

'We should have asked him to get sweets,' I whispered to Lisa.

'Aw, yeah. Why didn't we do that?' She made a face.

'Shouldn't be long!' Alan shouted from the kitchen. 'Come through and help me.'

We got up and walked slowly through to the kitchen.

'I didn't know what kind of pizza you liked,' he said, 'So I just got little cheese and tomato ones, but I bought some pepperoni that we can slice on top. Who wants some?'

He was holding a red-coloured sausage in one hand and, in the other, a sharp-looking knife. Where had that come from? I couldn't take my eyes off it and my heart was beating fast again. Was this what he would use to kill us with later?

'Not for me,' Lisa mumbled, and I shook my head.

He cut a slice of the pepperoni and ate it himself. 'There are plates in the cupboard.'

Lisa reached up to the cupboard he indicated and pulled out three plates. They were a bit dusty so she rinsed them under the tap then looked around for a dishtowel. The only one in sight had brown stains all over it and I wished she hadn't bothered. She carefully found a cleanish corner and used that to wipe our plates dry.

We stood waiting awkwardly as he sliced off pieces of pepperoni and my eyes followed the path of the knife as it arced through the air. He used the dishtowel to protect his hand as he pulled out a tray of oven chips and the pizzas. He placed one pizza on each of our plates then he chucked a handful of chips on top.

'There you go,' he said. 'Just what you asked for. Don't say I'm not good to you.'

As I took my plate, I wondered why he was bothering to feed us if he was going to kill us later. What was the point of that? He could have saved his money.

We carried our food back through to the sitting room and sat down on the sofa. I nibbled a few chips but couldn't face the pizza, which looked doughy and undercooked. Lisa had a bit of hers then put her plate down on the floor.

Outside it was getting dark and I began to get more frightened. If he were going to murder us, it would be after dark. Would he take us out of the flat to do it, or would he kill us here and sneak our bodies out?

He came through and sat on the floor in front of us to watch the television. He still seemed a bit agitated, and that made me more alarmed. I suspected that he was building up his courage to do something. He didn't talk to us at all and after a while, he got up and took our plates of uneaten food back through to the kitchen.

I looked at Lisa and whispered: 'What do you think he's going to do next?'

'Don't know.'

We listened to him crashing plates around in the kitchen. I strained my ears, wondering where he was going to put that knife. I was sure it hadn't been in any of the kitchen drawers when we searched them the day before, but if not there then where did he keep it?

Sitting waiting to see what he was going to do next was like being in the dentist's waiting room but a thousand times worse. Whatever happened, it was likely to be painful. There was nothing I could do to get out of it. My stomach kept gurgling and I pressed my belly hard, trying to stop it.

His footsteps came down the hall and he looked into the room.

'Charlene,' he said, and beckoned with his finger. 'Your turn. Come on.'

I felt as though all my muscles and bones were as heavy as lead and I had to struggle to move. Slowly I stood up and walked robot-like towards him without looking round at Lisa. I felt numb again, as if this was all a bad dream, or as if it was happening to someone else and not me. I was outside my own body and watching from somewhere far away as he closed the bedroom door behind us and pulled the t-shirt over my head. His smell was in my nostrils. I kept my head turned away so I didn't have to look at him.

11

Thursday night

Lisa

While Charlene was in the bedroom, I saw yet another interview with Keith on the telly. The interviewer asked: 'Where do you think Charlene is?'

Keith said, 'My theory is that she's at somebody's house and I'm hoping that's a safe place to be.' He kept hesitating as he spoke.

'What do you say to that person?'

'I say to them – please send them home.' He looked right at the camera with a pleading expression.

I felt a twinge of jealousy that Charlene's dad was doing so many appeals and my parents weren't. I wondered why that was. Keith was obviously just pushing himself forward in a way that my dad wouldn't know how to, even if he had thought of it. I knew he loved me – that wasn't in doubt. It was just that he was much more reserved.

I didn't wonder why Mum wasn't making an appeal. It was dads who were supposed to protect you from harm in the world, wasn't it? When I got hurt as a kid, it was always my dad I wanted. There was the time in reception when I fell in the playground and took the skin off my knees. I cried so much I missed my lunch. I remember the tender look in Dad's eyes when he got home that evening and took the bandage off to clean the wound for me. Even though it stung a bit, I felt safe with him looking after me.

Then there was the time when I went to an after-school art class and got stung by a hornet that was caught up in my hair. I felt something crawling up there and I put my hand up to flick it away and got stung across the knuckle, which was incredibly painful. Back at home, Dad had some cream – I don't know what it was – and when he rubbed it really gently around the sting, the pain went away. He had huge hands and that's why it was so sweet when he was being careful not to hurt me. He was super strict, and not one for teasing and mucking around like Keith, but my dad was a very kind, gentle man.

Just as I was thinking about Dad, an advert came on the television that was filmed underwater with lots of fish and dolphins, which was a coincidence because Dad kept a big tank of tropical fish at home. He loved his fish and would tell us all about them – their names, which part of the world they came from, what they liked and didn't like. I think it was from him that I got my ambition to swim with dolphins one day. He had explained what gentle creatures they were and told me some amazing stories about how they rescued human beings from shark attacks by making a circle around them in the water so the sharks couldn't get through.

The Bill came on TV. I was never normally allowed to watch it at home. It was a complicated plot, though, and

I lost track of it before long. I just couldn't concentrate on anything except what was happening to us now and worrying about what was going to happen next. There was no sound from the bedroom. I went over to the window and outside the lights were flickering against a jet-black sky. There was no moon visible, but maybe we were facing the wrong way. I could see a few cars going past in the street below but it was too far to try and attract attention. Everything about me felt heavy. It was as though there was a huge weight pressing down on my shoulders making it hard to do anything. I needed a wee but couldn't be bothered to go.

Time was dragging. Everything was wrong and horrible. How long could it possibly go on like this? First me, then Charlene, then me again; surely Alan would get bored of it before much longer. What did he like about forcing young girls to do things they didn't want to do? I just couldn't understand how that could give him pleasure. It was nice if you liked a person and they liked you back, and then you wanted to say lovely things to them and give them presents, but you couldn't force someone to be your friend by bullying them into doing things they didn't want to do. Alan seemed to think that the girls who came to his flat to play on the computer had wanted to do these things with him, but I doubted it. I bet they were scared of him, just as we were.

The programme had finished and a new one started when Charlene appeared in the doorway, like a ghost. She walked across and sat down on the sofa without looking at me or saying anything.

'Are you alright, Char?' I asked.

She just nodded.

'What did he do?'

'The same.'

Outside I could hear him pacing around now and I wished I had gone to the toilet earlier when he was still with Charlene, so I wouldn't have to bump into him. I was getting desperate, though, so eventually I stood up. I told Charlene what I was doing and she hardly reacted. She seemed very far away and caught up in her own thoughts.

Alan was sitting in the computer room. I think he was smoking because there was a strong smell of tobacco.

'What are you doing?' he demanded, turning round to look at me.

I pointed at the toilet door.

'Hurry up then,' he snapped. 'Don't be long.'

I finished as quickly as I could and scurried back to the sitting room. An idea had come to me and I wanted to put it to Charlene.

I sat on the sofa right next to her and whispered in her ear. 'Why don't we pretend we're really tired and go to bed now? We could pretend to be asleep. That might stop him trying to do anything else tonight.'

'OK.' She nodded. 'Will we put the TV off?'

'No, leave it on. He might come in to see what's happening if we put it off.'

We crawled into the single bed top to tail and pulled the covers up to our chins and closed our eyes. A short while later Alan came in but we both kept our eyes tightly shut and tried to breathe slowly, the way you do when you're sleeping. I could tell he was standing there looking at us for ages then he turned the television off and went away again.

I think I actually fell asleep after that, but not for long. A hand was shaking me by the shoulder and pulling back the covers.

'Come on, Lisa,' he said, pulling me up by the arm. 'I need you in the bedroom.'

When he had finished with me, he brought me back to the single bed and wakened Charlene, and it went on like that all night long. I'd get an hour or two of sleep and then I'd be taken next door and abused, and then back again.

Around about dawn, when he came in and started shaking me, I pretended I couldn't wake up. I kept my eyes tightly shut and made sleeping noises but he just slipped his arms underneath me, picked me up and carried me through. As he laid me down on the bed, I looked at the clock and it was just after six am. Didn't he need any sleep? I'd never known him to sleep during the whole time we were there. He was awake when we went to bed and awake when we woke up, and even if I stirred briefly in the night I could usually hear him moving around somewhere in the flat. I thought he must be an insomniac.

He got into bed beside me and pulled the covers over me and started putting cream between my legs. I wriggled to get away.

'You can't do that. I'm too sore,' I said.

'But I'm not letting you go until I've got it in,' he replied coldly.

I screamed as he tried to ram himself inside me and he put his hand over my mouth. He just kept moving me around and trying to put his willy inside me and if I screamed he would cover my mouth. When he was trying to rape me, there was a horrible expression on his face: his eyes were closed and he was concentrating hard, his mouth stretched in a kind of ugly grimace. It made my stomach turn with revulsion. The pain was worse than ever before. I felt as though I was being ripped in two. I couldn't feel anything except a sharp tearing pain.

'There you are,' he said at one point, and I guessed he had finally achieved his goal.

When I could, I turned my head and watched the hands of the clock going round and round, and tried to guess how long it could possibly go on for. One hour, two hours, three hours. I set milestones. I thought if I could just make it to half past maybe he would stop then. It carried on after half past, so I thought 'OK, he'll stop by ten to.' All the way through, I broke it up into those chunks of time and steeled myself to get through each one. I didn't think about Charlene, or Mum and Dad, or Nan and Granddad; I just thought about getting through the next twenty minutes.

I don't know how I survived those hours. I felt like a rag doll being tossed around cruelly. I felt like an object rather than a person. He'd stop for a while and play with himself or try to get me to play with him then he'd move me around and it would all start up again. The pain was worse than any pain I had ever experienced in my life before. I tried to do what Charlene said she did and distance myself from it but it was too harsh and immediate. I was Lisa Hoodless and an evil man called Alan Hopkinson was hurting me very badly. I wondered if I would be damaged for life.

Could you die of being raped? I had no idea. I wished he would die though. I hated him with a passion. How could he be getting pleasure from hurting me like this?

I felt even angrier when he stopped and stroked my face and told me how pretty I was. What did he think? That I would agree to be his girlfriend or something? The creep. The evil creep. I felt like punching and scratching his face, but I was too scared in case he hit me back.

It was six minutes past nine when at last he told me I could go. I stood up very carefully. My whole body felt broken. It chafed between my legs when I walked. I pulled the t-shirt on and staggered back through to the sitting room. Charlene looked up as I climbed into bed beside her, with my head beside her head.

'You've been gone ages,' she said.

Tears came to my eyes and I blinked them away fiercely. If Charlene could put up with it all without crying, I could do the same. 'He did it to me,' I said. 'It really hurts. I think he's torn me.'

She put her arm around me and we hugged. I was praying that he would leave us alone for a while now. I knew I couldn't take any more. I couldn't stand any more of that awful pain that seemed to fill my whole body.

He was bustling around outside, doing goodness

knows what. Charlene and I just lay there in each other's arms, hardly talking at all but getting comfort from our physical closeness. The curtains were still drawn and winter sunlight was streaming round the edges. He hadn't put the television on so we could hear every sound he made quite clearly: the toilet flushing, the flare of a match as he lit a cigarette, his footsteps shuffling along the hall, the computer booting up.

I think I dozed off for a while, exhausted from the broken sleep of the night before. Charlene was dozing as well. But we were both wide awake when we heard a sound we had never heard the whole time we had been in the flat: a loud, insistent banging on the door.

12
Friday

Charlene

The knocking was really loud. My first reaction was pure terror. I thought Alan might have invited some of his friends round to have sex with us, or maybe it was the man next door, the one he had told us wouldn't be as gentle as him. Lisa and I pulled the quilt right up to our chins and huddled against the wall. We heard Alan come out of the bedroom into the hall. He started pacing up and down but didn't answer the door.

There was another loud knock and then a man's voice shouted 'Police!' and Lisa and I looked at each other and grinned. It was the best feeling of my life. It was so good. Relief just spread through my body like warm sunshine.

But Alan wasn't answering the door. He stuck his head round the sitting room door and hissed at us: 'Don't say a word. Just keep quiet.' Then he went back to pacing in the hall and started swearing away under his breath. 'Shit! Fuck! Fucking hell!' He was using every swear word under the sun. The whole time we'd been there, we'd never heard him swearing before. He'd always been very well spoken.

Lisa and I were still smiling, but my smile began to fade as I realised he wasn't planning on opening the door. What if the police just gave up and went away again? We didn't know why they were there but if it were just a routine thing like a parking ticket, maybe they would decide to leave it.

There was another loud knock and another shout of 'Police!' Alan kept pacing and swearing and ignoring it. I don't know why Lisa and I just sat there doing nothing. We could have shouted out to the police to tell them that we were there and they could have broken the door down but we were still too scared of Alan – and to be honest, the thought never crossed my mind.

They knocked again and the warm feeling of relief I'd had was completely replaced by fear that they would turn around and go away and we would be stuck in that flat for ever. We were still prisoners, even though some potential rescuers were just ten feet away. So near and yet so far.

Alan sounded really upset. It was weird hearing him like that because he had never lost his calm during the whole time we'd been with him. He was muttering away and I suppose he was trying to decide what to do. The knocking went on for about five minutes altogether. Every minute I thought, 'Surely they're going to give up now' and my hopes would be raised when I heard the next knock and the next shout.

And then we heard Alan turning the key in the front door lock. I listened hard, not even daring to breathe in case I missed a single word.

'Good morning, sir,' a man's voice said. 'Are you Alan Hopkinson?'

He must have nodded because they carried on, 'We've had complaints about you from some local girls.' They gave the names.

Alan sounded nervous when he replied. 'Really? I can't understand what they would complain about.'

'We'd like you to come down the station to answer some questions,' the policeman said.

'What, now?' Alan sounded stunned.

'Yes, sir. We don't want to have to arrest you. It would be best if you come voluntarily.'

There was a pause then Alan asked, 'Can I just get a couple of things first? My tobacco and my wallet?'

'Certainly, sir.'

The police stayed at the front door and suddenly I got worried that he would go off with them and leave us trapped there without any food and we would starve to death. Still it didn't occur to us to shout out. We were too traumatised and exhausted to think clearly.

We heard Alan go into the bedroom and then he came back out to the hall. 'Oh, by the way,' we heard him say as if it was an afterthought, 'I've got the two missing girls from Hastings in the front room.'

That was it! We would be freed. I stood up and quickly pulled on my school trousers, which were on the floor by the bed. All I could think was that I didn't want the policemen to see me in that t-shirt with no knickers.

Seconds later, a police officer came into the room.

When he saw us huddled together on the bed, he grinned from ear to ear. 'We've been looking for you,' he said. Another policeman put his head round the door to look, and exclaimed 'Oh my!'

Lisa and I couldn't speak. We were too shaken up, I suppose. Then everything seemed to happen very quickly. The first police officer stayed with us, while the other one must have stayed with Alan in another room and radioed for assistance. We could hear the crackly radio noises out in the hall.

'Are you OK, girls?' the policeman asked, looking sympathetic.

We nodded.

Lisa picked up her school clothes to get dressed, but he said, 'Don't get dressed yet. We need you as you are for evidence. Don't touch anything for now.'

We sat on the bed looking at each other and smiling shyly, without talking. It seemed like only a few minutes before more police officers arrived – three or four of them at least. The place suddenly seemed full.

'We'll just take you down to the car now,' our first one said. 'We'll go to the police station and then I'm sure you want to see your families as soon as possible.'

One of them picked Lisa up and another one picked me up and they carried us out to the hall. I think Alan was in the kitchen at the time because I didn't see him again. When we got to the front door, I blinked in the bright light. It had been so dimly lit in the flat that I couldn't open my eyes properly in daylight any more. It was dazzling that morning. It was an amazing feeling to be free but intimidating at the same time because I didn't know what would happen next.

The policeman was really big and carried me effortlessly down the flights of stairs to a police car. It was only then I turned round and realised I couldn't see Lisa any more.

'Where's Lisa?' I asked in a panic. I wanted us to stick together.

'Don't worry. We'll be bringing her in a separate car. So you're Charlene Lunnon, are you?'

I nodded.

'Your dad is going to be so pleased to see you.'

I felt tears pricking my eyes and blinked them back. I didn't feel like talking. There were two policemen in the car, both smiling at me, but I felt as though I was in a dream. I felt as though I had been in the flat for months and months, even though it was just over three days since we'd been captured. And I wasn't happy about being separated from Lisa. I felt as though we should stick together, and was hoping we would be reunited when we got to the police station.

I was so glad I'd managed to put my trousers on before they told me not to. Poor Lisa must be sitting in her police car in that manky white t-shirt and no knickers. I looked out of the car window and there were shops and buses and people walking along without a care in the world, as if nothing had happened.

'We're taking you to Battle Police Station,' one of the policemen explained to me. 'We need to ask you some questions and then your dad will come and pick you up.'

I couldn't wait. I wished I didn't have to answer the questions, though. I didn't want to have to tell anyone about all the awful things we'd been through. Putting them into words would make them all seem more real, and I knew I would be embarrassed about it as well. But I realised that they needed evidence to send Alan to jail so he couldn't do that to other girls, so it had to be done.

We pulled up outside the police station and once again the policeman lifted me up to carry me inside because I didn't have any shoes on. There were loads of people milling about inside and it felt weird seeing so many faces. I was only used to Alan and Lisa. I felt safe there, but I just kept wishing they would bring Lisa so we could answer the questions together.

First I was taken into a room like a doctor's surgery and there was a nurse there, wearing a white uniform. She had a brown ponytail and the nicest, friendliest face I'd ever seen. She sat me down and explained that the doctor was just going to have a look at me to see if I was hurt. She explained that it would be just us in the room and a woman doctor. No men. I said that was OK.

First of all she examined my arms and legs, looking for marks, I suppose. Then I climbed up onto a bed with some white tissue paper on it and she held my hand as the doctor came in and started looking at me. It felt horrible when she touched me between my legs, but she kept talking all the time, explaining what she was doing, and she told me she had to take a swab. I think they were checking to see if there was some of Alan's sperm there.

After she had finished doing that, she took a blood test

and then she said, 'Are you hungry? Would you like something to eat?'

I nodded. I suddenly realised I was starving. My stomach was growling.

The nurse took me along a corridor to a room with a table and chairs in it. On the table there were plates with lots of sandwiches cut into little triangles and some chocolate biscuits as well.

'Help yourself,' she said, smiling. 'Have whatever you want.'

I picked up an egg mayonnaise sandwich and took a bite and it tasted delicious. I munched it down quite quickly and then I had a chocolate biscuit, but after that I felt full and couldn't manage any more. I looked at all that food and knew I should eat more because I'd hardly had anything for days, but it was as if there wasn't any more space in my stomach.

'I've had enough,' I said.

'That's fine. You can have more later.' She winked at me. 'Now, would you like to get dressed? Your dad has brought in some clothes for you from home.'

'He's here already? Can I see him?' How had he got there so quickly? He must have been sitting by the phone and got straight in the car when they radioed from the flat. Tears came to my eyes.

'Not quite yet. We need to ask you some questions first, but he's in the building waiting to take you home as soon as we've finished.'

I was desperate to see him and frustrated to think he could even be in the next room, but I had no choice but to do exactly as I was told. They were the police, after all.

Someone came in with a bundle of clothes. I looked through it quickly to see what Dad had chosen. There was my favourite yellow fleece, which I loved because it was so soft, and some jeans and trainers, underwear and socks. Comfortable clothes. I slipped them all on and it felt really good to be dressed normally. I was starting to feel like myself again.

'Are you ready to answer some questions?' she asked me.

'Yeah, OK,' I said. I wanted to get it all over with as quickly as possible so that I could see Dad and he could take me home. I wanted my old life back and to forget about everything that had happened in the last few days.

I was led along some corridors and into a cosy room that was like someone's sitting room with a big sofa and lots of toys on the floor. There were teddy bears and dolls, all of them for much younger children than me. I wondered what very young children could possibly be doing here. A policeman and a policewoman were sitting on the sofa with a table in front of them and they smiled when I came in. Everyone kept smiling at me.

'Where would you like to sit, Charlene?' they asked, so I chose a chair and sat down. Then they explained that we were going to be filmed while we were talking and that two other people would be watching the film in another room. I wasn't quite sure why but it didn't seem to matter so I didn't ask questions. I just wanted to get on with it. I was getting more and more impatient to see Dad.

'Can you tell us your name, please?' they began.

'Charlene Lunnon.'

'And your address.'

I just answered the questions as clearly as I could. I told them about the mushy potato in Cornfield Terrace and being shut in the car boot, and going to Alan's parents' house, and then being taken up to his flat. When they asked about what he had done to me, I think they were trying to be delicate and not upset me with their questions, but I just said it straight out: 'He raped me.'

'Do you know what rape means?' they asked.

'Yes, it means he put his willy inside me.'

'Where did he put it?'

'In between my legs.'

'How many times did he do it?'

I had no idea. 'Lots,' I said simply.

That wouldn't do, though. We had to go through each day of captivity with a fine-tooth comb and I did the best I could. When I told them about the night when he nearly pushed me off the cliff top, I saw them glance at each other with horror on their faces. The rest of the time they just kept their expressions unemotional and calm and friendly.

They kept going back over the same things time and time again. Sometimes they would go back and ask me yet another question about something I thought I had already answered and I was beginning to think it would never be over. I reckon I was probably in there for about two hours altogether. Finally they smiled and said, 'Would you like to see your dad now?'

I jumped to my feet eagerly. 'Where is he?' I had goosebumps on my arms.

They led me out of that room and along a corridor then they opened a door and there was Dad, and Philomena and Ceri-Jane and Mr Okrainetz, all sitting together.

Before I could even step into the room, Dad ran over, threw his arms around me and picked me up. He was kissing and cuddling me and when I looked at his face he was crying.

'I'm so happy you're back,' he said through his tears.

'I didn't run away,' I told him. I wanted him to know that straight away.

'I know, I know,' he said.

'It said on the telly that they thought we had run away and I was worried you might be angry.'

'Don't be silly.' He started crying even more. 'We just wanted you home safe and sound. Are you OK, Char?'

'Yeah, I'm fine,' I said. Then a thought came to me. 'How's Fluffy? Has someone been feeding her?'

I thought it was a perfectly reasonable question but the grown-ups in the room gave a funny kind of laugh.

'She's fine,' Dad said. 'We've taken good care of her.'

I couldn't wait to see her. That was the next thing. I wanted to play with Fluffy and sleep in my own bed and then I wanted to go back to school as if nothing had happened. It had been an awful experience but now it was all over and things could return to normal again.

I turned round as the policeman was carrying me out of the flat and saw Alan collecting his tobacco pouch from the bedroom. He was facing away from me, his shoulders hunched over, and another police officer was watching him from the doorway. I felt real hatred for him at that moment and hoped that would be the last time I ever saw him in my entire life.

As I was carried out into the daylight, the brightness made me squint. I felt a bit embarrassed about the fact that I had no knickers on under the t-shirt and it was bunching up where the policeman was holding me. I wasn't exposed but another couple of inches and I could have been. Obviously I was over the moon to be rescued but it was stressful as well, wondering what would happen next and where they had taken Charlene.

There were two police officers in the car – a man and a woman – and the woman explained that they were taking me to Hailsham Police Station. She said they needed to ask me some questions and then my mum and dad would come and pick me up.

I nodded. That sounded fine. I was in a daze as we drove through the streets of Eastbourne. It seemed strange to see people outside carrying on their daily lives.

'Everyone's been looking for you,' the policewoman told me. 'They even brought in the army.'

'I know,' I said. 'We saw it on the news.'

We drove in silence most of the rest of the way, then

when we got to the station the policeman lifted me and carried me inside. They took me to a room and someone appeared with a big Tesco bag full of chocolate. I could see Curlywurlys and Crunchies and all sorts.

'Is Char coming?' I asked. I thought I should share the sweets with her.

'You'll see her later,' someone said. 'Are you hungry?'

'Starving,' I said.

'What would you like to eat? We've got a kitchen here, so just tell us what you feel like.'

I went through into the kitchen and looked in the cupboards and picked out a tin of spaghetti.

'Would you like that on toast?' a woman asked, and I nodded.

She heated the spaghetti in a microwave and toasted some bread and put it on a table in front of me. I started eating and it tasted delicious, but after a few mouthfuls I felt full and put the knife and fork down.

'When can I see Mum and Dad?' I asked.

'We need to give you a quick medical check-up then ask you some questions first. It won't take long. Are you ready?'

I didn't like the sound of the medical check-up – I'm not keen on doctors – but I let them lead me down a corridor to a little room with a couch in it.

I sat down at the desk and the doctor asked me a few questions first, then she said that she needed to examine me. 'If you could just lie on the couch I'll do a quick physical examination and then you can get dressed in your own clothes.'

I got up on the couch reluctantly. 'I didn't bring my clothes from the flat,' I told her. 'I don't know what happened to them.'

'It's OK. Your mum has brought in some clothes for you,' she said.

'Is she here already?' I was amazed. They must have really rushed down.

'Yep. She's just waiting until you get through the procedures then she can take you home.'

That was a comforting thought. All I wanted was to get home as soon as possible.

The doctor pulled on some rubber gloves, pushed my legs open and said 'I'm just doing a quick swab.' I felt a scraping feeling and I screamed and curled my legs up. 'Don't touch me! It hurts too much.'

'I'm sorry,' she said. 'OK, I won't touch any more. Can I just have a look, Lisa, to see what's happened to you?'

I relented and let her open my legs again, and I lay staring at the ceiling, feeling exposed and humiliated as she made notes on her clipboard about what she could see.

'It's very swollen,' she said. 'Maybe I should see you again in a couple of weeks when the swelling has gone down and we can do the other tests then. Would that be OK?'

I agreed; anything to get this over with. 'Can I get down now?' I asked and she said that I could.

The nurse brought in a bundle of clothes for me to put on, but I was shy about taking the white t-shirt off with both of them watching.

'Can you not look?' I asked, and they both turned away.

I had a look through the pile. Mum had obviously just grabbed the first things that came to hand. There was a pair of my sister's white high-heeled shoes, some disgusting tight leggings and a bright yellow Adidas jumper with blue lines down it.

Oh, great! I thought. I'm going to look like a total idiot. It was the most embarrassing outfit I'd ever seen but I had no choice but to put it on.

Next, I was led to a room where they were going to question me. There was a camera, some chairs and a blue carpet. I felt a bit shy when I saw the camera but a woman stood up and came over to me.

'My name's Tracey Christmas,' she said. 'I'm going to be your liaison officer. That means I'm here to protect you and I'll be coming back to stay at your house for a while to make sure everything is alright.'

She seemed nice but I didn't understand. 'Why do you have to come to my house?'

'You know how celebrities have bodyguards?' I nodded. 'I'm going to be your bodyguard for a while because we want to make sure you are completely safe now. Nothing else is going to happen to you. I'm going to make sure of that.'

She grinned and I decided I liked the sound of having a bodyguard. I wasn't quite sure why I needed one, because I assumed they would put Alan in jail, but it would be nice to feel completely safe.

'They won't let Alan go free, will they?' I asked.

'No. That won't happen,' she assured me.

Tracey Christmas and another man were going to be the ones asking me questions, but she explained that we were being filmed and other people were watching us from the next room. And then I just had to tell them the whole story, day by day, of what had happened. They made me be very specific about it all. Every time I said something like 'He did it again,' they would ask 'Did what again?' and I had to say, 'He put his penis in my vagina.' I was embarrassed saying those words, and I think I had a little embarrassed smile on my face. They weren't words I would normally use but Tracey explained it was important to be absolutely clear for the court case when Alan was on trial.

The questioning took hours. At first I was trying my hardest to remember every single thing and give them all the information I could, but towards the end I know I was getting really tired. They wanted to go over and over the same things time and again until I was going crazy.

'Can't I stop now? I've told you everything,' I kept asking and they would say, 'Just one more thing' and we'd be talking for another half an hour.

Eventually they said I could come and see Mum and Dad. Tracey led me down a corridor and pointed to a door. 'They're in there,' she said.

I thought to myself: I mustn't cry – and then I opened the door.

Dad jumped out of his chair and came running over to me and there were tears streaming down his cheeks. He looked terrible. 'Hey!' he said. That was all.

It was the oddest thing, because I had never seen my dad crying before. He's not very big on showing his emotions but he was certainly showing them that afternoon. He gave me a hug and then Mum came and gave me a hug as well, and then I couldn't hold it back and I started crying. We all stood there for a while, hugging and crying, and then Dad wiped his eyes and cleared his throat and said 'Why don't we all go home?'

Tracey Christmas was taking us in her car. I asked if Mum could sit in the front because I wanted my dad in the back with me. I hadn't been allowed to bring my orange quilted jacket – they were keeping all my clothes and my schoolbag for evidence – so it was perishing cold when we got into the car.

I hugged myself and said 'It's freezing in here.'

Straight away, Dad took off his big cream-coloured coat and wrapped it around me, then he kept his arm around me all the way home. Mum was chatting away about all the people who had been worried about me: the aunts and uncles and cousins who'd been phoning wanting news the whole time I was missing. We've got quite a big family. She said we would have to call and speak to them all as soon as we got home, but that was the last thing I felt like doing. Dad didn't say a word. He just sat there with his arm around me, which felt very peaceful and calm.

It was getting dark outside – I think it must have been about four or five o'clock in the afternoon – when we turned into our road. I saw lots of cars parked and my first thought was: Oh, all the family's here! Our driveway had some cars in it so we had to pull up outside the gate, and Tracey Christmas came round to open my door.

All of a sudden bright lights started flashing everywhere and I realised the whole front garden and the street outside was full of photographers – loads of them. Flashbulbs were going off and people were shouting questions at me. 'How are you feeling, Lisa?' 'Is it good to be home?'

Tracey Christmas told me to walk behind her and hold onto her belt, keeping my head down. Dad followed right behind me, so we were this peculiar procession, with me in the middle still all wrapped up in Dad's massive coat, and flashbulbs going off all around, and people shouting questions and jostling each other. I thought it was exciting. It had never occurred to me that the press would be there but I hoped my picture would be in the newspaper the next day and I smiled when I looked up at the cameras.

When we got inside, my sister Christine came up and gave me a hug, then my brother gave me a quick pat on the back looking embarrassed at all the emotion being displayed around him. My mum's friend Alyssum Fitzpatrick was there looking after baby Georgie so she got up to give me a hug as well and then I picked up Georgie and gave her a cuddle.

I went up to have a look at my bedroom and was amazed to see that Christine had kept it pretty tidy while I was away. It felt as though I'd been gone for a long time – weeks or months even – and it was hard to remember that it wasn't even four days.

Alyssum had brought me a present of lots of colouring

books and felt pens, so I just sat downstairs in the sitting room and started colouring in. Mum was on the phone making call after call to all our relatives and she tried to get me to go on the line and talk to them but I didn't really feel like it. Everything felt unreal and I tried to stop myself thinking about what I'd been through by focusing very hard on colouring in the books as perfectly as I could, choosing the best colours and making sure I didn't go over the lines.

No one asked me what had happened, and that seemed odd. I didn't want to tell them but I thought they would have asked rather than just ignoring it. Mum was saying on the phone to people, 'She's absolutely fine!' and I thought, How do you know? You haven't even asked me. I wished I could go round to Charlene's and talk to her about how strange it all was to be back home with our families as if nothing had happened. No one else in the world could understand what I had been through except her.

Granddad came up just to give me a big hug. My nan popped over with her husband and then the grown-ups were all drinking champagne. Everyone was worried because I said I didn't want any tea, but I just wasn't hungry. I hated them fussing over me in that careful way, as though they were tiptoeing round me, trying to say the right things.

I had a bath that evening and it was still very sore between my legs, which was a harsh reminder that things weren't normal no matter how much I wanted them to be.

When we went to bed, I made Christine turn off the

light as usual, because her bed was closer to it, but I couldn't sleep. My mind was buzzing with thoughts: Would I be in the newspapers in the morning? What would happen to Alan? When would I see Charlene again? When would I go back to school? What would my friends say?

My dad was very strict about bedtimes. We had to go to bed whenever he said and we weren't allowed to get up again, but I could hear Mum downstairs chatting and giggling with Alyssum and I decided to take a risk and sneak down.

I went into the front room and said, 'Mum, I can't sleep.'

'That's alright,' she said, smiling. 'Come and join us.'

I looked at the clock and it was midnight. Mum and Alyssum were drinking wine and I think they were a bit merry because they kept laughing at silly things. Dad was already asleep upstairs. I just got my colouring books out and started doing more of my pictures, keeping them as neat as I could. I wanted to fill in all the pictures perfectly. I wanted it to be the best colouring I had ever done.

Charlene

We had to wait in the police station for a couple of hours before we were allowed to go home, which was frustrating because I just wanted to get out of there. There were lots of kids' toys in the room where we were waiting, just as there had been in the interview room. I think it was some kind of children's suite. Dad and Philomena and Ceri-Jane were telling me about what had been going on while I was away but no one asked what had happened to me. I got the impression that the police had warned them not to ask me questions.

'I was out in the car looking for you every single day,' Dad told me. 'And I made lots of appeals on the telly.'

'Yeah, I know. I saw them.'

'Did you?' he smiled. There were still tears glinting in his eyes. 'That's why I did so many because I was hoping you would see at least one and you'd know we were looking.'

'I think I saw them all,' I said. 'We watched a lot of telly.'

'The Spice Girls did an appeal for you,' Ceri-Jane told me. 'Baby Spice did it on the night of her birthday party. She said "Please come home, Lisa and Charlene."'

'I don't even like the Spice Girls any more,' I told her, and they all laughed. It was true; I'd gone off them recently.

Mr Okrainetz looked as though he didn't know what to say. 'I'm so glad you're back,' he kept saying. 'When I came to England for an exchange year I never expected anything like this to happen.'

He seemed very emotional, which was embarrassing because he wasn't even family.

After about ten minutes of chatting with everyone, I felt as though I'd never been away. I put everything that had happened in the flat into a box in my head and locked it away. I just stopped thinking about it.

'Can I have some chips?' I asked. 'I'm starving.'

Straight away, Dad leapt up and ran out to get me some chips from a nearby chip shop. I think if I had asked for the Crown Jewels that day he would have gone and got them for me. When he came back I sat and munched my way through them and they were the most delicious chips I had ever tasted in my life.

I don't know what we had to wait around for, but at last we got word that we were allowed to go home. We were being driven there in a police car because Dad didn't have his own car with him. As we turned into the little cul-de-sac where our house is, I couldn't believe my eyes: the whole street was totally mobbed with reporters and cameramen and TV vans, all of them there just to get a picture of me arriving home.

'Charlene! Over here!' they were shouting before I even got out of the car.

A policewoman had come with us and she got out of the car first then told me to keep my head down and hold onto her belt as we walked towards the house. She put a coat over my head so I could hardly see where I was going.

'No matter what you do, don't let go of my belt,' she instructed.

The walk from the car to the house was a bit crazy. Some of the reporters were trying to grab me to get the pictures they wanted and the policewoman had to push them away. One of them trod on my foot and it really hurt. I thought it was mental that they wanted my picture so much. Everything felt strange and unreal.

When we got inside, a man with dark hair and glasses came over and introduced himself as my police liaison officer, Paul Hilton. He seemed really nice. 'I'm going to be staying with you for a bit just to make sure you get settled in again properly and feel safe,' he told me.

Dad explained, 'Paul's been staying at the house with us since you disappeared, keeping us up to date with all the news about the search.'

'Where did you sleep?' I wanted to know. I wondered if he had been in my room, because obviously it had been empty. I didn't like that idea.

'I've just been sleeping downstairs on a sofa,' he said, as if reading my mind. 'I don't need to stay overnight any more now. I'll come round in the daytime, until you're settled.'

After that I ran straight up to my room to see Fluffy. Her cage had been cleaned out and she had fresh water and food, but she was sound asleep in her bed. I wakened her and lifted her out to stroke her but she didn't look particularly pleased to see me. Her eyes were only half open and she was very sleepy so I put her back again.

My room was all neat and tidy and there were some presents for me laid out on the bed: new blue pyjamas with little Dalmatians on them and a pink fluffy dressing gown and fluffy Dalmatian slippers.

'I got these for you,' Philomena said, watching from the doorway. 'I thought they looked nice and cosy.'

I stroked them and they certainly felt very warm and comfy.

Dad made me chicken nuggets and chips with lots of ketchup for my tea and then I had a bath and got changed into my new pyjamas and dressing gown. Paul Hilton was in the sitting room when I came back downstairs, so I showed them off to him and he smiled and nodded approval.

'Very nice!' Then he said, 'All the reporters are still camped outside.' I looked out the window and I could see the huge lights they'd set up in the street. 'They're not going to leave until they get a picture. I wonder if you feel up to just going out on the doorstep with your dad for a couple of minutes?'

'Yeah, that's fine,' I said. I felt completely normal, as if nothing had happened. To tell the truth, I was enjoying all the attention.

Dad and I went to the front door together and all the flashbulbs went off at once, like an explosion.

'How does it feel to be home, Charlene?' someone shouted.

'It's great,' I said.

'Keith, what's it like to have her back?'

'It's unbelievable,' he said. 'It's a miracle that she's home safe and sound. I'd just like to say thank you to everyone for all their help and support over the last few days, which we really appreciate.'

I stood there in my new pink dressing gown grinning from ear to ear and enjoying myself hugely. We stayed outside for about ten minutes so that they all got the pictures they wanted for the morning papers.

After that, I asked if I could phone Lisa. I wanted to

find out if there were lots of photographers at hers as well.

'Yeah, it's mad,' she said. 'They're blocking the driveway and right the way down the street.'

'Did you go out to see them? I just went out on the doorstep in my pyjamas.'

'No, Dad won't let me. You know what he's like.'

'Are you going back to school on Monday?' I asked. I was keen to go back, not because I missed the lessons or anything but because I wanted things to be normal again.

'I'd like to but Mum says I've got to have a couple of weeks off. What about you?'

'I haven't asked Dad yet.' I called through to the kitchen to ask him. 'When do I have to go back to school, Dad? Lisa's having two weeks off.'

'You should have two weeks off too and go back on the same day as her. Is that alright, sweetheart?'

I passed that back to Lisa. 'Will I see you in the week, though?' she asked. 'I miss you.'

'Miss you too,' I said.

After our conversation, I was suddenly exhausted. I looked out the window and all the photographers were still there, even though we'd let them take their pictures earlier. I waved at them and all the flashbulbs started going off again. I couldn't keep my eyes open. It was only about seven o'clock but I was just so tired that I decided to go up to bed. I love my own bed and it was the best feeling ever to snuggle down under the duvet and pull it up to my chin. Dad came to give me a goodnight kiss and he said that if I wakened I could just come back downstairs again, but I fell asleep really quickly and slept soundly right through till the morning.

Our ordeal was finally over, and against all the odds we had survived.

PART 2

13
Charlene

Over breakfast the next day, Dad told me that a photo-call had been arranged down on the beach. The press and TV people wanted even more pictures of us and they wanted us to answer a few questions as well.

'Wear something nice,' Dad said, so I chose my chocolate-brown velvet skirt and matching jacket, with my best black shoes with little heels.

We drove down the road to the beach just near our house and when I got out of the car, I saw Lisa straight away. She was just wearing black trousers and a blue zip-up fleece. I ran over to give her a hug, and said, 'Why didn't you get dressed up? They're going to take our photo.'

'No one told me,' she said. 'You look really nice.'

Her brother James came over to give me a quick, embarrassed hug. All the cameras were filming us already.

'Stand over here, girls,' someone shouted, so we both went and stood where they wanted us to and I put my arm around Lisa. Two reporters came up and gave me a big white rabbit with a pink ribbon round its neck, then they gave Lisa a teddy bear.

'How does it feel to be home?' someone asked us.

'Um . . . fantastic!' I said.

Another reporter came up and handed me a David Beckham lunchbox and I turned round to make a face at my dad. He's a Manchester United supporter and he was always trying to get me to support them as well but I hated football. I couldn't understand why they would give me a football lunchbox, unless, maybe, he had told them I liked Man U, which was just the kind of trick he might play.

'What have you been doing since you got back?' someone shouted.

Lisa answered this time. 'I've been cuddling my mum and dad and we had a little chat, then I had a nice hot shower.'

'Did you miss school?'

'Yeah,' Lisa said. 'And all my friends. And my boyfriend.'

I couldn't believe she had said that in front of all the journalists. I turned to look at her, grinning, my mouth open with surprise. She giggled.

'What's your boyfriend's name?' someone asked.

'Stevie,' she said, all embarrassed now. I wondered what he would say when he heard his name on the TV like that. I didn't think he'd be very pleased.

'What did you miss the most, Charlene?' they asked.

'My dad moaning at me,' I said, and turned round to grin at him. Every time I looked at him, I just felt so happy to be back. He was such an amazing person and I loved him so much.

When they had finished all their questions, Lisa and I hugged goodbye and arranged that we would speak later. In the car on the way home, I examined the toy rabbit they had given me. It was huge, almost half as big as me.

'All the journalists seem really nice,' I said.

Paul Hilton snorted loudly.

Dad turned round. 'Don't you believe it,' he said. 'They might be giving you presents today but a couple of days ago they were blackmailing me. They found out that I used to be a drug addict and said they were going to write a nasty story about it unless I gave them an interview for their paper.'

I was shocked. 'What did you do?'

'I did the interview, of course. I was actually talking to them when Paul got the phone call to say that you and Lisa had been found. They didn't know for sure it was you at first. They just phoned and said two girls matching your descriptions had been found in Eastbourne.' His eyes filled with tears at the memory. 'Paul told me to grab some clothes for you and we jumped straight in the car to go to the police station. I knew right away it was you. It had to be.'

He reached round from the front seat and gave my hand a squeeze, blinking back his tears. I didn't feel at all emotional about it now. It was all in the past as far as I was concerned.

When we got back to the house, all the journalists had gone from our street.

'Can I go to the shop to get some sweets?' I asked.

'Sure,' Dad said, looking at Paul. 'I'll give you some money.'

'I'll come with you,' Paul said. 'It's my job to stick with you for now, if you don't mind.'

I didn't mind at all. Dad gave me two pounds, which would buy a lot of sweets, and as we walked down the road, I realised I would have been a bit too nervous to do it on my own. I knew Alan must be in jail now, and wouldn't be allowed out, but what if there were other men like him in the world? What if Alan's next-door neighbour came looking for us? Or what if one of the reporters came back and started pestering me with horrible questions I didn't want to answer?

Paul was very easy to talk to. He asked if I wanted to get any more animals, like a rabbit or another hamster, to keep Fluffy company. I told him I didn't think she would like that very much but that I was saving up my pocket money to get a Furby.

'What's a Furby?' he asked, and I laughed. How could anyone not know that?

'They're furry creatures that can talk to you. They laugh and sigh and dance and if you talk to them they answer back.'

'So they speak English?'

'When you first get them they're only babies and they speak Furbish, but as they grow up they learn to speak English.'

'How do they do that?' He sounded amazed.

'The same way that human babies learn English, I suppose.'

The very next morning when Paul Hilton arrived at

our house, he was carrying a plastic bag. 'I've got something for you,' he said, handing it over.

I looked inside and there were not one but two Furbies – one brown and one pink.

'But they cost thirty pounds each!' I gasped.

'Money's not the most important thing, is it, Charlene?' he smiled at me. 'We all know that now.'

That weekend, everyone was making a huge fuss of me. Every single person who came to the house brought me presents. Both my half-sisters rang me, and the first thing Carol said was 'What did he do to you, then?'

Dad overheard her and grabbed the phone away from me. He seemed really angry. It was obvious he'd been told that I wasn't to talk about it and no one was to ask me anything, which suited me fine.

'Sorry, love,' he said afterwards. 'Carol's a bit nosy and I thought it might be awkward for you.'

'I wouldn't have told her anything anyway,' I said.

'You'll have your first appointment with the counsellor next week, after school,' he told me.

I frowned. I didn't like the sound of that. 'Do I have to do counselling? I don't want to.'

Paul Hilton reassured me. 'Don't worry. The counsellor will be a really nice lady and you'll enjoy yourself there.'

On Sunday, two days after the police rescued us from the flat, Dad announced that Auntie Vera and Uncle Harry were coming down for the afternoon. I was really pleased because I loved my Auntie Vera and was dying to give her a big hug.

They were due around two o'clock and when I heard the car pulling up, I ran outside to meet them. As soon as I looked into the car, though, my heart sank. They'd brought Bert with them.

'What's he doing here?' I blurted out first thing as the car doors opened.

Uncle Harry looked puzzled. 'Bert's been really worried about you and he specially asked if he could come down to see you today. Aren't you pleased?'

I put my arms around her waist and hugged her, burying my face in her coat so she couldn't see my expression. I felt sick to my stomach just looking at Bert, with his ugly face and his pervert's smile. I decided to try and ignore him all day until they left. I'd just keep well out of his way.

We went in and sat in the sitting room. All the adults had cups of tea and were chatting away.

'I wanted to get you a present,' Auntie Vera said, 'But I didn't know what you'd like. So why don't we go out on a girls-only shopping trip this afternoon and get you some new clothes? You can show me where your favourite shops are.'

'OK,' I agreed happily.

'I can drive you if you like,' Paul Hilton said. 'I have to stick with her for the time being,' he explained to Auntie Vera.

So far I had managed to avoid even looking at Bert, but as I stood up to go to the kitchen for some juice, he grabbed hold of my arm and pulled me playfully down onto his lap.

'Don't you have a hug for your old friend Bert?' he asked.

I froze. I couldn't scream and struggle to get away without the whole story coming out in front of everyone and I didn't have the courage for that. I sat stock-still, my face a mask. Surely they should all have been able to see how much I hated being on his lap. Wasn't it obvious?

Still holding me firmly by the arm, Bert pulled a cushion in front of me and his fingers started stroking my boob behind it, moving up and down, while he carried on talking to the grown-ups as if butter wouldn't melt in his mouth.

I felt sick and disgusted and angrier than I had ever felt in my entire life. I pushed his arm away, jumped up off his lap and ran out of the room. I couldn't believe it. Two days after I'd been released from being held captive by Alan, here was Bert trying to stroke my boob in front of everyone.

I ran upstairs to my bedroom and threw myself down on the bed, absolutely seething with rage. Although Bert had never tried to rape me, as far as I was concerned what he did to me was far worse than what Alan did. He was left to babysit for me and my aunt and uncle trusted him to behave himself – but he hadn't. How could he do that to a young girl?

I could still feel the place where he had touched me. It felt contaminated. I pulled off my sweater and got changed into another one that wouldn't have the imprint of his fingers on it.

At that moment, I knew for sure that I hated Bert

more than I would ever hate Alan. At least Alan was in jail for what he had done. Bert should be going to jail as well, for all his creepy 'games' and perverted habits. He had ruined my childhood and for that I would never forgive him. Not ever.

14

Lisa

When we got to the beach on Saturday morning, the day after we were set free, Charlene came charging up to me. 'What are you doing?' she asked. 'We're having photos taken. You haven't dressed up or anything.'

'I didn't know,' I said. 'Nobody told me.' It was really good seeing her back to her normal bossy self again after she had been so subdued in Alan's flat. It felt as though the old Charlene was back, the one who was in charge and usually told me what to do instead of the other way round.

My brother James was messing around, holding up a finger to the journalists when Mum and Dad weren't looking, so I had to keep an eye on him, and answer the questions everyone was asking, and it all felt weird. As soon as I said to the TV cameras that I'd missed my boyfriend Stevie I thought, Oh no, why did I say that? He's going to kill me. It had just slipped out.

The photo-call was over quickly and I had to say goodbye to Charlene again when I would have preferred to spend the afternoon sitting chatting with her in her room – not talking about Alan but just being friends again without all that stuff in the way. It seemed as though my life wasn't my own any more, because every hour was booked up with people who wanted to come and visit us to say 'welcome back' to me. The doorbell was ringing every five minutes.

All the visitors brought flowers until the kitchen was filled up with so many bouquets that we ran out of vases and they were piling up in the sink. I got some great presents as well. My godmother Angela, who was my mum's cousin, brought me a cute cuddly toy dog that I called Toffee. Mum and Dad bought me the video of the musical *Cats*, which I had wanted for ages, and I was really chuffed about that. Then Tracey Christmas brought me two Furbies, which was fantastic. She said Charlene had told her bodyguard Paul that we both wanted some, and that she thought when we got together maybe our Furbies could talk to each other. I felt like the luckiest girl in the world.

No one asked me anything about what had happened in Alan's flat and I was trying my best not to think about it but at night, when the lights were off, all the memories came flooding into my head. I started having nightmares that I was back in the flat, trying to get away from him but I knew I couldn't. He was on top of me and I couldn't breathe. I could smell his smell. In one of the nightmares he was holding a knife to my throat. I'd wake up panting, my throat tight with fear until I heard Christine's calm breathing in the next bed. The darkness of the room disturbed me, so I asked Dad if I could maybe leave the light on.

The next day, Dad went to a lighting shop in town and picked out a gorgeous lamp. The base was a pink ceramic pig and there was a pleated shade on top. I loved it and called it my 'piggy lamp'. From then on I left it glowing beside my bed at night. The nightmares continued but at least I wasn't lying in pitch black when I woke up. That lamp really helped a lot.

On the Monday, three days after we were rescued, the headmistress of our school came round for a chat. I liked her. She smiled a lot and talked quietly, but I had to sit and be polite and to be honest I could have done without it.

'Everyone at the school was praying for you,' she said.

What was I supposed to say? 'Thank you,' I mumbled at last.

'All the children have been told that they are not to ask you any questions when you get back. I'm sure you don't want everyone pestering you for details. If anyone does get inquisitive, you should just tell Mr Okrainetz or me and we will deal with them. We want to make this as easy as possible for you.'

'Thank you,' I said again.

She started chatting about the work the class had been doing while I was away, and the new school uniform we had to get because the old one had been kept by the police as evidence. I sat politely nodding and thanking her and reassuring her that I was fine. She meant well, but I felt very awkward talking to her after everything we had gone through. I didn't know how much she knew or what she thought about it all and I didn't want to know. I was dreading the first day back at school when I imagined all the pupils and teachers would be staring at us and wondering what had happened to us, but we'd just have to get through that before things could go back to normal.

Later that afternoon, Tracey Christmas came in to have a word with me. 'Lisa, I think you should know that Alan's lawyer has released a statement in which he apologises to you and Charlene.'

'He's done what?' I could hardly speak, I was so surprised. You can't kidnap someone and do all those things to them and then just apologise. What did he think? That we would just say 'It's OK, don't worry about it'?

She saw my expression of horror and hurried on. 'It's good news, because it means he's going to plead guilty at this trial. That means that you don't have to go along and answer questions at the court case. The evidence you gave when you were questioned at the police station will be enough.'

'Will he go to jail?' I asked.

'Definitely. For a very long time.'

I shrugged. 'That's OK then. Does Charlene know?'

'Paul will tell her.'

I felt strangely unmoved by this news. I remembered the morning in the flat when Alan apologised to us. His words meant nothing. I didn't want any of his pathetic self-pity or attempts to justify what he had done. Basically I just wanted to know for sure that he would get a long jail sentence and then I wanted to forget all about him.

'If you want to ask me questions, you can do it any time,' Tracey said. 'No matter what.'

'Actually,' I said, 'there is one thing.' I'd heard her mentioning to Mum the day before that she had once lived in Australia and I'd been dying to ask her about it.

She laughed when I asked my question, and then she started telling me about the beaches off Perth where everyone goes surfing and there are nets to keep out the sharks; about the markets and outdoor cafés in Fremantle; about the bushland that surrounds the town; and the beautiful Swan River flowing through it all.

'I've always wanted to go to Australia,' I told her.

'Well, you must do it one day,' she said. 'It's unforgettable.'

I liked Tracey a lot and felt very comfortable with her around. I was relieved that I didn't have to go out anywhere on my own because I was still feeling a bit anxious that something else could happen. And her presence also meant that the family were on their best behaviour: no arguments at the dinner table, or James and Christine stealing my money, or Dad yelling at us to be quiet. I liked it that way.

As the week went on, I got fed up with all the grown-up visitors to the house and wanted to see my own friends, but of course they were at school during the day. Mum took me round to Charlene's one day but not for long and we had to sit downstairs and talk to the grown-ups who were there instead of going off on our own.

'Why don't we throw a little party for your friends next

weekend?' Mum suggested and I thought that was a great idea. It would be nice to see everybody in my own home for the first time without prying ears listening in to our conversations. I thought that I would probably tell my closest friends what Alan had done to me because I trusted them, but I would ask them to keep it to themselves. I didn't want it to go any further. I called to invite Charlene to the party and we discussed between us who should be there until we had agreed on a final guest list of ten girls from our class. I decided we could make little cakes together and Mum bought the ingredients for me along with things to decorate them.

Charlene arrived early on the day of the party to help me get things ready. Mum had got mixes for both strawberry and chocolate cakes, and some edible paper pictures that you could stick on the top. I made strawberry cakes and stuck Dennis the Menace pictures on top of them. Charlene made chocolate ones but some of hers didn't work out and she got really annoyed about it.

'I thought you said you had greased these trays, Lisa.'

'Yeah, I did.'

'Not very well,' she said. 'You've ruined my cakes. And the icing is too runny as well – it's just dribbling off the sides instead of sitting on top.'

I couldn't understand why she was being so grumpy but I tried to smooth things over by offering her one of my cakes as a swap.

We took all the food through to the sitting room and set it out on the table. When the other girls arrived, their mothers dropped them off and left. We more or less had the place to ourselves as Dad was upstairs with my brother and sister and the baby, while Mum had gone out. At first, we just messed around, eating the food, chatting about news from school and commenting on each other's clothes. Then Samantha, my old friend from nursery school, took the plunge and asked what was on everyone's mind.

'Are you going to tell us what happened then?' she asked me. 'What did he do?'

I looked at Charlene and we caught each other's eyes for a moment, then shrugged.

'Let's all get under the table and we'll tell you,' Charlene suggested.

We crawled underneath the long tablecloth and huddled in the space there and started telling them about our ordeal.

'The first day he took me into the bedroom but he didn't take Lisa,' Charlene said. 'He took me lots more than her at the beginning.'

'On the last morning, I was in there for about three hours, though,' I butted in.

'What did he do to you?' someone asked.

'He raped us,' Charlene said and there were gasps of horror.

We told them all the dramatic bits of the story: about how he had snatched us on Cornfield Terrace, about being smuggled around in the sports bag, about going to his mum and dad's and then to his place, and about the strange experience on top of the cliff.

'Did you think he was going to kill you?' someone asked.

'Definitely,' Charlene said. 'He was definitely going to kill us if we hadn't been rescued.'

It was odd to be talking about it like this, turning it into a sensational story to entertain our friends. I was aware that we were showing off a bit, boasting about everything we'd been through, but they were such an appreciative audience it was hard to resist. They were gasping with horror and saying 'Poor you!' or 'Oh my God!' and we were totally the centre of attention.

'What did you do when he was raping you?' someone asked.

Charlene answered before I could. 'Lisa used to cry all the way through but I just focused my mind on something else and concentrated on that so I didn't have to think about it. It was easier that way.'

Maybe it was true, but I didn't like the fact that it made me sound like a crybaby. 'You cried too,' I said.

'No I didn't,' she insisted crossly. 'I never cry. When have you ever seen me cry?'

It was true that I couldn't remember ever *seeing* Charlene cry but I had definitely *heard* her crying in the flat. I didn't argue any more though. It became clear to me that afternoon that Charlene wanted to be the one who told the story of our time in captivity. I didn't mind. It was all the same to me. Besides, having told my closest friends that Saturday afternoon, I didn't plan on telling any more people.

'You won't tell anyone else, will you?' We made them

promise before they left that afternoon that they would keep everything to themselves. It was naive, of course. Ten-year-old girls were never going to be able to keep such a huge secret, especially as the months went on and allegiances changed, friendships drifted and some former friends were declared enemies. Before long, the entire school would know we'd been repeatedly raped by a disgusting paedophile. That afternoon, though, I felt very close to my little group of best friends and very lucky to have them. Huddled under the table with them all close by, it felt as though I really was back home and getting on with my life – and that's what I wanted more than anything else.

15

Charlene

It was two weeks before Lisa and I went back to school. On the first day back, Paul Hilton took me there, while Lisa came with her bodyguard Tracey Christmas. I felt very shy walking through the playground. Everyone was staring at us but no one came up to say anything because they'd been warned not to at school assembly. They weren't supposed to ask us any questions at all.

I had a brand new school jumper, black trousers with a thin little pinstripe, new shoes with little heels, a black padded jacket and a new schoolbag and lunchbox. I was particularly pleased with the schoolbag, which was an orange inflatable rucksack, and I swung it proudly.

First we had to go to the headmistress's office and she asked if we were alright, and if we were sure we were ready for this. I said yes, we were, because to be honest I was fed up with all the fuss and bored with sitting around at home. I was sure that as soon as I got into the classroom and sat down at my normal desk, it would be OK.

When we walked in, Mr Okrainetz said, 'Hello, Lisa. Hello, Charlene. Welcome back.'

We took our seats, Paul and Tracey left, and Mr

Okrainetz started a lesson, but I was conscious of people staring and whispering. I hated that. I would much rather they had called out to ask whatever they wanted rather than staring at me and talking behind my back.

I turned to one girl and asked 'What's your problem?' and she blushed and said 'Nothing.'

Lisa was two desks behind me and I caught her eye. She gave a sympathetic smile. She was going through the same thing herself.

By breaktime I had decided to put on a confident front. I've always been good at bravado. Everyone seemed to expect me to be a nervous wreck, constantly breaking down in tears, and that wasn't how I felt at all. I didn't want to be treated any differently than the way I'd been before it all happened. I was still the same person deep down, although I suppose I felt more worldly-wise than the rest of my classmates. They were still just kids and I had been through a life-changing experience since the last time I was in that classroom.

Lisa and I stood together in the playground and lots of people crowded round us, chatting about things we had missed at school, who was going out with who, new clothes some girls had bought and so on. They all wanted to be friends with us, even if they weren't allowed to ask about our ordeal. They probably hoped that we would trust them enough to tell them some details in private. Everyone was bursting with curiosity that day.

Lisa was going off to a different lesson after the break, but she squeezed my hand as we trooped indoors and whispered 'You OK?' I grinned and said, 'Yeah. You?'

She nodded. We were allies in all of this. We would put on a united front.

At lunchtime, all the girls in our class wanted to sit near us. They were jostling just to get close. I began to enjoy the attention. We were being asked to parties and for play-dates, and everyone was admiring my new schoolbag and shoes. By the end of the day when Paul and Tracey came to pick us up, it was clear to Lisa and me that we were suddenly the most popular girls in the whole school. We giggled to each other about it.

'It's amazing what being kidnapped can do for your popularity!' she said.

'They just want the gory details,' I commented.

'Well, they're not getting them from me.'

'Me neither.' I was pushing the experiences with Alan as far back in my head as I could and avoided consciously thinking about it at all, so the last thing I wanted to do was answer questions about it from nosy classmates.

Unfortunately, there were two events soon after my return to school that brought it all to the forefront again.

First of all, a teacher handed me a letter as I was walking along a corridor at school.

'This arrived at the office for you, Charlene,' she said.

I knew there had been lots of letters arriving at home from members of the public who wanted to tell me how happy they were I'd been rescued and wish me well in getting my life back to normal. I'd read a few of them and thought they seemed like very nice people, so I assumed this letter the teacher gave me was another of the same.

I ripped open the envelope and started to read. The writing was very messy.

'Dear Charlene,' it said, 'I think it is really good that you were abducted by Alan Hopkinson because you have learned lots of things about sex and you've lost your cherry. I'm going to find you and abduct you myself now and we'll do much more things than Alan ever did to you, just you wait and see.'

I was so shocked, I slumped against a wall feeling breathless. My chest was tight as if I was going to have an asthma attack. I looked up and down the corridor, scared that whoever sent the letter might be there, coming to get me already.

I looked down at the scrawled page again. Underneath there was a picture of a pregnant woman with a big arrow pointing to it, and the words said 'This is what I am going to do to you.' There was no signature at the bottom.

For a minute, I couldn't think what to do, then I ran towards our form classroom where Mr Okrainetz was sitting marking.

'Look what came for me!' My voice was trembling as I handed it over.

He read it quickly, then folded it in half. 'I'm so sorry, Charlene. Who gave this to you?'

I told him the teacher's name.

'She's made a big mistake. We were told that on no account should any letters be passed to you.'

It took me a minute to understand what he meant. 'Why? Have there been other ones?'

He was flustered. 'Look, you'll have to talk to your dad about this. I think they've had one or two at your house and that's why they warned the school. The world is mostly full of good people, but there are a few very sick ones and it's been your misfortune to come up against one here.' He tapped the letter.

'I don't understand why anyone would write that to me. Are they really going to try and find me?'

'I doubt it very much. It's just some sad, crazy guy who wants to make himself feel important by getting in contact with you. No doubt the police are on his trail already and they'll catch him before long. In the meantime, you're safe while you're at school and you've got your police protection officer at home. Please try not to worry.'

Another thought occurred to me. 'Has Lisa had letters as well?'

'I believe she has,' he said.

I wondered why she hadn't mentioned it. Maybe they hadn't told her about them. I went off and found her in the playground. 'Have you been getting letters from some sick guy who says he wants to do things to you and make you pregnant?'

'You what?'

'I got one just now, sent to the school.' She looked really shocked.

'That's sick! Imagine doing that! Are you OK?'

'Yeah.' I shrugged. The letter had upset me, but now it

was gone, I was going to shut it out of my mind, just like all the other bad things. After all, a piece of paper couldn't hurt me and I believed Mr Okrainetz when he said that the police were after whoever had written it.

Mr Okrainetz had phoned my dad and he showed up at school soon afterwards. Lessons had started so I stood out in the corridor to talk to him.

'I'm sorry you had to find out,' he said, giving me a hug and looking sad. 'I was keeping it back from you so that you weren't worried. It's just one sick bloke sending his nasty letters and the police are close to arresting him. You mustn't be frightened. Paul Hilton is going to stay with us until he's behind bars so you're not in any danger.'

That was reassuring. Paul was a big, calm, capable man; the kind you would want to find yourself next to if you were trapped in a building on fire. I couldn't imagine any situation he couldn't deal with.

'Are you alright?' Dad asked.

'Yeah, I'm fine,' I said. I meant it. Now I was over the shock of reading the letter, I wasn't scared at all.

'Good.' Dad hugged me again and smiled comfortingly. 'There are lots of complete prats in the world, Char. This man is one of them. Don't let him get to you.'

So I didn't.

A couple of weeks later, Paul told me they'd arrested the man who was sending the letters, who turned out to be a taxi driver. I was glad to know that he'd been found. I wasn't curious about him but at least I knew now there was no way he could come after me.

All I wanted to do was forget about everything that

had happened with Alan, but life seemed to be conspiring to make me remember it. Our story had slipped off the front pages not long after we'd been found; there was a happy ending now and everyone could relax and enjoy the outcome. But at school, I was still the object of curiosity and not a day went past when I wasn't reminded in some way of what I'd been through.

Then I had to start the counselling.

It was about a fortnight after I was rescued, around the same time that we went back to school, that my dad drove me to a specialist children's hospital where the sessions would take place. We were taken to a bright, colourful room with comfortable furnishings where there were lots of toys – dolls and teddies and so forth – and a blackboard and coloured chalks. Then my dad said that he would wait for me outside and I was left alone for a few moments, standing in the middle of the room and wondering what would happen next. The door opened and a woman with curly ginger hair and glasses came into the room.

'Hello, I'm Penny,' she said. Her skin was tanned and she had loads of little freckles all over so that there was almost more brown skin than white. I liked her smile, which seemed very genuine. 'Have a seat. How are you feeling today?'

I sat down on one of the soft armchairs. 'Fine.'

Penny sat down opposite me, with a file open on her lap and a pen in her hand so she could take notes. She looked me straight in the eye. 'How are you finding it being back at school? Is everyone being nice to you?'

'Yeah,' I said. In fact, I was a bit upset that day because I'd heard that some boys had made up a rumour that Lisa and I had been chained in a basement the whole time we were held captive, and they were spreading it round the school. That annoyed me. I just wished they would mind their own business, but it didn't occur to me to tell Penny about it.

'You've been through a huge trauma,' she said kindly. 'You must still be feeling very shocked about it.'

'No, not really.'

'It would be only natural if you felt a bit scared and a bit sad about it too.'

I shook my head.

'Do you mind telling me about it, so I can understand what you went through?'

I shrugged, and answered her questions as briefly as I could without being rude. I just gave her a general outline of what had happened but insisted that I didn't feel upset or sad about it, because that was the truth – I didn't. When I thought about it now, I felt nothing at all. What no one seemed to understand was that I didn't want to think about it if I could possibly help it.

She pointed out some paper and crayons on the table and asked me to draw a picture of Alan's face. I'm not very good at drawing but I did my best to try and make it look like him, with his long face, combed-over hair and droopy moustache.

Penny seemed surprised when I handed the picture to her. 'He looks quite ordinary,' she said. 'Wasn't there anything about him that looked as though he wasn't a very nice person? What about his eyes? Or his mouth?'

I think she wanted me to draw him with evil monster eyes and blackened teeth and a scowl, but that's not how I remembered him. I just drew what I'd seen: a sad, unsmiling but quite normal-looking man.

'How do you feel about him now?' she asked.

'Nothing, really,' I said. 'I'm trying not to think about him.'

'I can understand why you would want to do that,' she said, 'But it's important not to bury your feelings. Sometimes if we feel angry and we don't express it, it turns inwards and eats away at us and makes us depressed. I'm here to make sure that doesn't happen to you. Over the next few weeks, we're going to talk about absolutely everything that happened in there – maybe even things that you feel a bit ashamed or uncomfortable about now – and that way we can make sure that you don't have any emotions that turn inwards and cause you harm.'

'Will you tell my dad everything I tell you?'

'Not about your feelings, no. But if there are any things that might affect the court case against Alan Hopkinson then I would need to tell the police or your dad. Any legal things, or things that might cause harm to you or another person. Is that OK?'

'When is the court case?'

'We don't know yet. I'll tell you when it's happening but you don't need to go. You heard, didn't you, that he is pleading guilty? That you don't have to go to court?' I nodded. 'How did that make you feel?'

I shrugged. 'I don't care. I would have gone to court if I had to.'

'You're very brave, Charlene,' she said. 'Usually it's a good thing to be brave because it means you are confident in life. But sometimes people pretend to be brave on the outside and inside they're actually feeling scared and sad.'

She obviously wanted me to break down in tears and admit that I felt scared and sad. She was gazing into my face with a lovely, kind expression, inviting me to tell her anything I wanted. But I wasn't going to lie just so she got the answers she was expecting.

'I don't think I'm being brave,' I said. 'The truth is that I feel absolutely fine and I just want to get on with my normal life. I don't hate Alan; I just want him to go to jail so he can't hurt any other girls. I'd rather not talk about it any more because I would rather forget about it. It's not brave, though. It's just what feels best.'

She nodded and wrote something down in her file. 'OK,' she said. 'That was a great start, Charlene. I'll see you again same time next week.'

My heart sank. She was obviously a very kind woman but I would rather have had my nails pulled out with pliers than sit there telling her about my 'feelings'.

'Do I have to go back?' I nagged Dad on the way home. 'I don't need it, really I don't.'

'Yes, you have to go back,' he said firmly, and I could tell he wasn't going to budge. Sometimes with my dad there was no point in arguing, and that was one of those times. I'd have been wasting my breath.

16

Lisa

I still hadn't had the dreaded police medical examination and it was hanging over me like a dark cloud. On the day it was arranged, 6 February, Mum and Tracey both said they would come along, so that comforted me a bit but it had hurt so much the last time that I was really nervous about it.

At first the police doctor, Dr Morris, just chatted to me and asked me how I was doing. She asked if I was still sore between my legs and I said that it was much better. Then she said she had to do a blood test and I went berserk. I hate needles. Can't bear them. It's a full-scale phobia with me.

'No, I won't do it!' I screamed and leapt out of my seat.

The doctor looked serious. 'I know you're frightened, Lisa, but you'll need to be as brave as you can. There are a few reasons for this test, but one is that we need your DNA for the court case against Alan Hopkinson. Do you know what DNA is?'

I had a vague idea, but no matter what it was for, I was still determined they weren't going to plunge a needle into my arm. Tracey and Mum were trying to calm me down and they got me to sit in the seat again. Mum had her arm around me and Tracey held my hand, but then I saw the doctor lifting the needle.

'Get off!' I yelled, and jerked my arm out of Mum's grasp.

'We also need to check you haven't picked up any infections,' the doctor explained. 'We can run some tests on your blood to find out.'

I reckoned I would rather just take my chances with infections than let her stick a needle in me.

In the end I was resisting so hard that they gave up. Tracey took swabs from my mouth with cotton buds so they could test my DNA that way, and the doctor said they'd just have to keep an eye on my health for the next few months. She told Mum that it was important I was seen by my GP if there were any unusual symptoms at all.

Next, it was time for her to examine me. Charlene had told me that it was sore but bearable when she had her test done at the police station. Either she was braver than me or she hadn't been hurt so badly because I found it horribly painful when Dr Morris started poking and prodding at me. I started crying.

Mum stroked my hair and said, 'It'll be alright,' and I was thinking, It's certainly not alright! Just leave me alone. Mum still hadn't asked me anything about what happened in Alan's flat. I think she couldn't face thinking about it, and I was glad because I didn't want to discuss it with her, but in the doctor's surgery that day it must have been pretty obvious to her what I'd been through.

The doctor was making notes on a clipboard. 'It's still

quite swollen but there are no tears and it's looking a lot better than it did last time I saw you,' she said, smiling at me. 'You're being very brave.'

I didn't feel brave. I felt angry. It always annoyed me when people said I was being brave. What did they want me to do? I had no choice about the things that were happening to me. I was still a child and I had to do as I was told.

At last it was over and we could go home again, but a couple of days later it was time for me to start my counselling. Charlene had started a few days earlier and she'd told me what to expect: that they wanted you to talk about your 'feelings' and tell them you hated Alan and so forth. Like her, I didn't want to do any of that. I just wanted to forget about him.

Dad drove me to the health centre and we waited until my name was called, then we both went into the room. There was a blonde woman inside, quite good-looking, with a nice smile. She stood up and shook hands with us both, saying, 'I'm Patricia. It's very nice to meet you.'

'I'll just wait outside,' Dad told me and I felt a bit panicky.

'Can't you stay?' I asked.

'That's not how it usually works,' Patricia told me. 'It's better if I can talk to you on your own. There might be some things you wouldn't feel comfortable talking about if your dad was here, because you didn't want to upset him, but it's important that you feel you can say anything to me. Why don't we give it a try without your dad this first time and see how we get on?'

'OK, sweetheart?' Dad asked.

I was doubtful but I nodded slowly.

'I'll be right outside. Come and get me at any time if you want to.'

After he left, I sat down on a chair and looked around. There were toys in a toy box in the corner and coloured posters all over the walls.

'Have you talked to anybody yet about what happened to you?' Patricia asked me first.

'I told the police all about it.'

'Not your mum or dad?'

I shook my head.

'I think you'll find it will be a relief to go through it all with an adult. Maybe I can help you to understand some things that might be puzzling you about your experiences.'

'I'm not puzzled.'

Patricia shifted in her chair, keeping up her concerned smile. 'There are different ways we can work. I quite like playing games and painting pictures. We'll try to make it fun when you come here. Maybe we should start by painting a picture today. Do you like painting?'

'I prefer drawing,' I said.

'Oh.' She looked around the room. 'I don't have any coloured pencils here, but I can get some for next time.'

'I can use a normal lead pencil,' I volunteered, wondering what she wanted me to draw.

'No, the colours you choose are very important. Could you maybe try to use the paints this time? I'll get pencils for next week.'

'OK,' I agreed. 'What do you want me to paint?'

She was putting a big sheet of paper on the table, and setting out the paints. It was a kids' painting set, where you had to dip your brush in water and rub the paint to get colour. 'I want you to paint a picture that shows me how you are feeling. Just paint whatever comes into your head.'

That sounded like a stupid idea. How could you paint feelings? I was feeling absolutely fine – just frustrated with all the people who kept harping on about things.

Patricia was waiting for me to start. I picked up the brush and began painting a girl sitting in a room but I soon realised it wasn't working out. The perspective was all wrong. It looked like a kid's painting. I didn't want her to think that's all I was capable of because I was quite proud of my art skills so I loaded the brush with black paint and scrubbed it all out with great sweeping strokes.

'It wasn't working,' I explained, and was irritated to realise that tears were filling my eyes.

'You must feel quite angry just now,' Patricia said in a gentle voice. 'A very bad thing has happened to you through no fault of your own.'

I started crying, and at the same time I was annoyed with myself for crying.

'It's OK,' she said. 'It's going to be alright.' She passed me a box of tissues and I took one and blew my nose loudly.

She continued. 'We're going to draw some pictures and chat about things and help you to feel less angry and less sad.'

'Next time,' I asked, 'can my dad stay in the room? I'd rather he was here.'

Something changed in her face. She was disappointed in me. 'I don't think that's such a good idea.'

'I'd really like him to be here,' I pleaded.

She was reluctant but finally said, 'If you're sure that's how you want it, we'll give it a try.'

I nodded, and wiped my eyes with a tissue. I didn't want Dad to see that I'd been crying because I was worried about upsetting him. He didn't say much but when we were at home he always wanted to be in the same room as me, and his eyes followed me with a kind of haunted expression. That's how I could tell that my abduction had almost been harder for him than it had been for me. He looked shattered, as though he'd been in a car accident or something. I knew that Charlene's dad Keith had taken leave of absence from his job because he couldn't handle going back just yet. I think my dad would have liked to do the same but the council wouldn't let him. They had both aged a lot in the three days we were missing. There seemed to be a lot more lines on Dad's forehead and around his eyes.

When my session with Patricia was finished I went out and told Dad that I had decided I wanted him to sit in with me in future and I think he was pleased. 'Whatever you want,' he said. 'We'll do it your way.'

When I saw Charlene later and told her that Dad was going to be at my counselling sessions, she was amazed. 'But you won't be able to talk about things like sex with him there. It'd be embarrassing.'

'I don't want to talk about sex,' I said.

'Counsellors like all that stuff,' she told me. 'Sex and dreams. They always want to know your dreams.'

I was still having nightmares almost every night in which I was back in the flat again. Alan was either a menacing presence in the next room, or his weight was pressing down on top of me. I'd wake up with my heart pounding and it took me a while to get back to sleep again.

'I'm not telling her my dreams,' I said. 'That's personal. I'm getting fed up to the back teeth with people asking me about it.'

The first day Charlene and I were back at school, everyone had crowded round us but no one dared to ask anything because they'd been warned not to. But by the second day, people were dropping things into conversation – 'Oh, I heard he had a gun'; 'I heard you were chained up in a cellar'. Stupid things like that. We usually just snapped at them to shut up and stop being idiots. Stevie, my boyfriend, had seen the TV coverage of the photo-call on the beach and he was very embarrassed that I had mentioned his name. He would hardly even come near me that week in case anyone teased him about it.

Gradually, as the days passed, things got back more or less to normal, except that everyone wanted to be our friend. 'Can I sit beside you in music?' one would say, and another would go, 'Will you be my partner at gym today?' or 'Do you want one of my sweets?' If I liked them, I just agreed. I'd always had two or three close friends in the past but suddenly I seemed to have about twenty! I knew it wasn't all real friendship and that they just wanted to be associated with me because of what I'd been through, but I was happy to go along with it if I liked them. Charlene had the same thing going on. My only regret was that I missed it just being the two of us, the way it had been before. I missed walking to school with her and stopping to buy sweets, and gossiping on our own in the corner of the playground.

I told myself it would all calm down soon and things would get back to normal – but I couldn't have been more wrong.

On the Friday of my first week back at school, a special needs teacher called Mrs Bourne came to our classroom. 'Lisa Hoodless?' she said. 'Your mum is here to see you. Can you come with me?'

I wondered what Mum wanted, then I guessed that maybe she had come to pick me up early because I had some appointment or other.

Mrs Bourne went to Christine's classroom next and we fetched her as well, then she led us both to the tiny special needs classroom. Mum was standing by the window and she turned to look at us with a very funny expression on her face. She seemed very tense and jumpy.

'Sit down, girls,' Mrs Bourne said. 'Your mum has something to tell you.'

There was one big table in the middle of the room with chairs arranged all the way round it. Christine and I sat next to each other at a corner and Mum came and crouched beside us on the floor. She looked terrible. I hadn't a clue what was going on.

It was ages before she even said anything. She just looked from one to the other of us as if she was trying to pluck up the courage.

'You know I love you both very much, don't you?' she began.

We nodded.

'The problem is that I haven't been getting on very well with your father. You've probably noticed that we've been arguing a lot.'

I hadn't noticed anything more than usual. She and Dad had always argued as far back as I could remember.

'The thing is . . .' She bit her lip, then the words came out in a rush. 'I've met someone else. His name is Tom. I'm going to go and live with him and your dad will bring you up now. I'll see you every weekend, though.' Her voice trailed off as she saw the horrified expressions on our faces.

'But, Mum, you can't!' I exclaimed.

'The decision is made, Lisa. It won't be so bad, though. You'll see.'

'Is it because of me?' Christine asked in a little voice. 'Is it because I was naughty?'

'No, of course not, silly!' Mum gave a fake kind of a laugh.

'Is it because I was kidnapped?' I asked. I started crying and Christine joined in.

Mum put her arms around us both and gave us a big hug. 'It's not your fault. It's just Dad and I can't get on with each other.'

Suddenly I remembered a dream I'd had earlier in the

week. I'd dreamt that Mum and Dad had a big argument and Dad took us away to live in a new house. It was like a mansion with a black-and-white checked floor in the hall and a big spiral staircase. The following morning I had told Mum about my dream and she gave me a really funny look as though she was going to cry.

'What's the matter? What have I said?' I asked.

'Oh, nothing, nothing,' she replied.

But it seemed as though my dream had all been true.

'When are you going?' I asked. Christine was sobbing so much that she couldn't even speak so I had to be the one asking the questions.

'Today. I'll be gone by the time you get home from school. That's why I thought I'd better come here to explain. Your dad will make your tea for you tonight, but I'll see you at the weekend sometime. Don't worry. It will all be fine.'

'Please don't go!' I cried. 'You can still change your mind. Just don't do it.'

She was stroking my hair. 'You'll understand when you're older, Lisa, that sometimes grown-ups have to do these things. I'm sorry. I've got to go now.'

'What about Georgie?' I asked suddenly. 'Are you taking Georgie?'

There was a pause. 'No, your dad will look after her.'

That was really serious if she wasn't taking Georgie. How would Dad manage to look after a baby when he had a job?

She gave us one last hug then stood up and hurried out of the room without looking back. Christine and I clung to each other, sobbing our hearts out, while Mrs Bourne tried to think of comforting things to say.

'You'll see your mum really soon,' she said. 'You'll probably have a bedroom at her new place and you can choose things for it. That'll be fun, won't it?'

Poor woman! She didn't know what to do with us. There was nothing she could have said to make things remotely better. As soon as the first fits of sobbing subsided, she walked us back to our classrooms.

I went in and everyone looked up. It must have been obvious that I'd been crying. I think Mr Okrainetz knew something about it because he was really nice to me. I sat down at my desk, still crying quietly. The girls who sat closest to me leant in and I whispered to them what had happened. Charlene stood up and came over to give me a hug. No one seemed to know what to say. None of their mothers had left them and gone off to live with another man, someone they'd never met.

It was the worst thing that had ever happened to me in my life. The experiences in the flat with Alan were nothing compared with this. My own mother was leaving me. I didn't know how I was going to carry on without her. It all seemed totally unreal.

17

Charlene

I couldn't believe it when Lisa said that her mum was leaving them, just a couple of weeks after we were released from our ordeal in Alan's flat. I was old enough to know that marriages do break up sometimes, but the timing couldn't have been worse. Everyone else in the world was buying us presents, cooking our favourite meals and making a big fuss to help us get over what we'd been through. I was still being treated like royalty at home, but now Lisa had another huge life change to come to terms with.

She sat sobbing her heart out in the classroom that Friday afternoon but there was nothing any of us could do or say to make things better. The way she was crying was worse than the way she had cried when we were kidnapped. It was as though she had been ripped apart. I was shocked because I'd always thought her mum was a nice woman and I would never have guessed she could do something like that.

I phoned Lisa that evening after dinner to see how she was doing. Her voice was very hushed because she didn't want her dad to overhear.

'It's just weird,' she said. 'Mum has taken all her clothes and stuff. She must have been planning it for ages. She must have had it planned even before we were kidnapped.'

'How's your dad?'

She sighed. 'He hasn't said anything about it. He just made us our tea and we all sat and ate it in silence and now he's in the kitchen clearing up. Do you think I should say something to him?'

'I don't know.' I was totally out of my depth. Lisa's dad never talked about feelings or anything. He was a nice bloke, but very quiet and unsociable. 'When are you seeing your mum again?'

'I don't know and I don't care,' she said – but I knew that wasn't really true.

'Do you want to come up to mine tomorrow?' I asked. 'To get away from it all?'

'I don't know,' she said doubtfully. 'I feel I should stick around and look after Dad, even if he doesn't seem as though he needs it just now. I'll give you a call though.'

I was disappointed. Since we were rescued, Lisa and I had hardly been on our own at all. We just grabbed snatched moments at my place or at school. It wasn't her fault – other people kept crowding round, wanting to sit beside us or play with us in the playground – but I sometimes got very jealous. She was supposed to be *my* best friend, not anyone else's. If she went and sat beside someone else in the lunch hall, I'd get a little twinge of jealousy, like a knot in my chest.

'I feel like I hardly ever see you any more,' I complained.

'I know,' she said. 'Me too. It's just for now that these people are all over us. They'll give up soon enough and we can go back to how we used to be.'

Things weren't going back to normal soon enough for me. One playtime, when Lisa was huddled in a corner chatting to another couple of girls, the knot of jealousy was causing a bitter taste in my mouth and an aching in my chest. A horrible thought came into my head: Alan was following her, not me, that morning. I only got into the car to try and protect her, then I got the worst of it when we were in the flat. He raped me more. So she owes me now. She should be my best friend and no one else's.

As soon as I had thought it, I was ashamed of myself. It wasn't Lisa's fault we were kidnapped, any more than it was mine. It wasn't her fault that I was more physically developed so Alan had focused on me at first. She hadn't actually done anything wrong.

But once the thought was there, it was like a poison that infected me. I couldn't help being a little bit tetchy with Lisa when I spoke to her later.

'I don't know what you see in her,' I said, referring to the girl she'd sat beside at lunch. 'She's a complete moron.'

'I know,' Lisa agreed. 'She's a bit boring to talk to.'

'What were you two talking about earlier?'

She frowned. 'I can't actually remember. All nonsense, probably.'

'You were talking nonsense as well, were you?' I snapped.

She looked at me, surprised. 'What's the problem, Char?'

'I just can't stand that girl and I don't know how you can spend time with her.' As soon as I had said it, I felt bad. 'Anyway, forget about it. What are you doing later?'

She groaned. 'Going home to help my dad get the dinner ready. Then probably helping him to do some ironing. I have to take over Mum's role because he can't manage everything on his own. He's given up his job to look after us but it's all too much for him.'

And then I remembered what a horrible time Lisa was having and tried to put my poisonous thoughts out of my head once and for all. 'Poor you!' I gave her a hug. 'Do you want me to come down and help you with the ironing? I'm pretty good at it.'

'I'd love to ask you,' she said, 'But I don't think Dad would let me have anyone round just now. He doesn't even like it when Granddad comes up any more.'

After school, I watched her as she walked off towards her house. Her shoulders were slumped and she seemed so sad that I wished I could wrap her up in cotton wool and make it better. I'd never heard of your mum leaving you before. Wasn't it supposed to be dads who ran off with someone else, not mums?

I'd lost my mum as well, of course, but it wasn't the same. I could never hug or talk to mine ever again – but at least I knew that she hadn't left me deliberately. She was doing everything she could to get me back at the time she died, whereas Lisa's mum had chosen her new bloke over her husband and children. I couldn't imagine what that must feel like.

Next time Lisa was chatting to someone else at break-time, or sitting next to someone else in class, I swallowed the lump in my throat and turned to talk to the person beside me instead. I had to try to be grown-up about this for Lisa's sake.

I was still going to counselling once a week but it didn't occur to me to tell Penny about my mixed-up feelings about Lisa, even when she asked how we were getting on. I told her about Lisa's mum leaving and how sorry I felt for her, and I said that we had promised each other that we would be friends for life and no one would ever split us up. I didn't say that I was starting to feel as though I was losing her and it made me very angry and very lonely at the same time.

I could tell I was a big disappointment to Penny. She made me tell her the whole story of the kidnap over and over again and she questioned my feelings about it at virtually every session. And I would always say, 'I don't have any feelings about it.'

We talked about my family background as well, so she knew all about Mum dying and the various foster parents I'd lived with before I came to stay with Dad. One day she suggested we should make up my family tree, and she asked me to bring in any old photographs we had at home. I didn't have pictures of my brothers, of course, and I only had two or three pictures of Mum, but I had a few of Carol and Rose and their kids, and Dad gave me lots from his side of the family. Penny brought in a huge sheet of paper and we pasted down the pictures of everyone, drawing in the links between them. I didn't mind at all when she asked me about my sisters or my mum – I just didn't want to talk about Alan.

One day, while I was sorting through some old papers in my bedroom, looking for photos, I came across a letter I'd received from social services in 1997, just after Mum died. In it, they explained why I had been taken away from Mum's care when I was younger, they told me about my other living family members, and they said they thought it was better that I remained in the care of my aunt and uncle while my dad sorted out his drugs problem. At the bottom of the letter, I had scribbled in childish handwriting, 'Bert is a pervert'. It was a shock to see it there. Of course, I hadn't shown that letter to anyone else but I must have been secretly hoping someone would come across it and ask why I had written that. As it turns out, no one had.

My anger with him was still white-hot. Whenever Penny asked me whether I felt angry with Alan, I answered truthfully that I had no feelings about him, but I thought to myself that Bert was the one I really felt angry with. Over the weeks, I started trying to decide whether to tell her about Bert. The one thing that stopped me was that I knew she would have to tell Dad and I was worried that he wouldn't believe me. That would have been the worst thing of all. He might think I was lying and just trying to get more attention.

Alternatively, what if he did believe me? He was still so

upset about me being kidnapped that he hadn't been able to go back to work and I didn't want to make things worse for him.

And I remembered that Bert had always said that if I told, people would think I was a slag. Was that true? Would they think I had gone along with it? In the early days, I had probably been quite flirty with him, in the way that little girls can be, because I liked the attention he paid me. Would everyone think I'd been asking for it?

I weighed up the pros and cons. Sometimes I thought I would tell Penny but when I got in there I just didn't have the courage. Lisa was the only person I could talk to about it and she kept urging me to tell so that Bert could be punished.

'He should be in jail, just like Alan,' she said, and I agreed. But I couldn't find the guts to do it.

Then one day, after I had been seeing her for a couple of months, Penny said she couldn't understand why I wasn't opening up to her. 'You never cry, although a terrible, terrible thing has happened to you. I don't believe you when you tell me that you haven't been affected by it. A grown man had sex with you against your will and made you scared for your life. You would have to be a robot not to be affected by that. Where have all your feelings gone, Charlene? Why are you so numb about it?'

The words suddenly came pouring out. 'If you really want to know, basically it was nothing new for me. It had been happening to me for ages before Alan kidnapped me.'

She looked really startled. 'What do you mean?' she asked.

'There was this guy at my aunt and uncle's house who used to have sex with me all the time. He didn't rape me but he did lots of other things. As far as I'm concerned what he did was much worse than what Alan did.'

I noticed Penny had tears glinting in her eyes, which I thought was odd. 'Who was he? What did he do to you exactly?'

I told her the whole story, and she listened and had to blow her nose into a tissue at one stage. She seemed very affected by it, and the great thing was that she obviously believed me straight away and didn't think I was a slag. Once I started talking about it, it was a relief to tell someone – a grown-up – at last.

'I think what Bert did was ten times worse,' I told her. 'So that's why I'm not so affected by Alan.'

'I can see why you would feel that way,' she said. 'He was in a position of trust. And you were much younger at the time.'

'Yeah, I was only six when he started doing stuff. I was tiny.'

'And you haven't told anyone else?'

'Only Lisa.'

'This sheds light on a lot of things for me,' she said. 'It's very brave of you to tell me. But now there are more brave things to do. I know it's difficult but I'm afraid your father has to be told.'

I looked down at my shoes. I'd been pretty sure she would say that.

'Do you want to tell him or will I do it?' she asked.

'You do it,' I mumbled.

'I'll call him in just now.' He was waiting outside the room. 'Do you want to wait here?'

I said I would sit out in the waiting room until they had finished. I didn't want to see his face when he heard the news.

Dad looked very puzzled when Penny told him she needed a word in private. I sat on a chair and scuffed my shoes backwards and forwards on the linoleum floor, my stomach all tensed up. What if he didn't believe me? But then, Penny had believed me straight away so perhaps Dad would too. And if he did believe me, what then? What would happen next?

I felt as though I was going to be sick with the tension of waiting. And then I heard the door opening and Dad came out. He just walked straight over and I stood up. He hugged me really tightly, then he said, 'I always had a bad feeling about Bert. I should have trusted my instincts at the time. I'm so sorry I didn't protect you, sweetheart.'

'It's OK,' I mumbled, embarrassed.

Penny wanted us to go back in to her office for a bit and it was only then I realised how upset Dad was. He was trying to hide it from me by blowing his nose into a big handkerchief that covered his face, but I could tell he was crying and that made me feel bad. I hated upsetting him.

Penny asked him what he was going to do next.

'I'm going to see my sister and brother-in-law,' he said. 'I'll drive up first thing tomorrow morning. And then hopefully she'll come to the police with me to turn him in.'

'They'll want to talk to you after that,' Penny said, turning to me. 'Don't be afraid, though. Just tell them the story exactly the way you told me and I know they'll believe you. No child makes up something like that.'

I supposed she was right. If Bert hadn't done it to me, I would never have dreamt that any grown man might want to have a pee on top of a child or lick her between her legs, so I couldn't have made it up if I tried. I still couldn't understand it. Penny had winced when I told her these details.

Dad was trying to be calm in front of me, but when I was in bed that night I heard him talking to Philomena downstairs. 'That fucking bastard!' he yelled, sounding angrier than I'd ever heard him before. 'I could tear him limb from limb.'

'You won't do anything silly, will you?' Philomena pleaded.

'I won't, but only because that girl upstairs needs me to look after her, so I can't afford to go to jail. Otherwise, I'd fucking hammer him. I'd kill him.'

I was petrified to think about what might happen the next morning when he saw Auntie Vera. I was told I had to go to school as normal but I was really shaken up. As soon as I could, I pulled Lisa aside and told her what I had done.

'Oh my God!' she kept saying, over and over again. 'Well done for telling, though.'

She was really sweet that day, keeping an eye on me at

lunch and breaktimes and passing me some nice notes in class, saying 'Keep your chin up. It will all be fine.'

Dad came to pick me up from school at quarter past three. He had the car with him, so I got in the front seat and waited for him to tell me what happened.

'I've been up to London and seen your auntie and uncle,' he told me. 'I've got Bert's address and everything and I've called the police. They want us to go down to the station now and make a statement.'

'What did Auntie Vera say?' I asked nervously.

'She was very shocked. She couldn't believe it had been going on under her own nose all that time without her knowing anything about it. I think she's also sad that you didn't tell her so she could have stopped it.'

'He said no one would believe me,' I explained.

'I know, sweetie, but that wasn't true. They would have believed you. The police will believe you. We'll put that man behind bars, just you wait and see.'

When we got to the police station, I was taken up to an interview room and two officers took my statement.

I told them the whole story, just as I had told Penny. I told them about the 'games' Bert made me play and how he'd get huffy with me if I didn't do what he wanted. I told them how he always said that it was a normal thing to do, that his sisters had done it to him when he was younger. And I told them I felt he had ruined my entire childhood. I loved my auntie and if it weren't for him I would have enjoyed staying there. I told them that I hated him and wished he was dead, and that I wanted him to be punished for what he had done.

They asked lots of detailed questions and made me use the proper names for body parts, like 'penis' and 'vagina', but I was used to all this after my last police interview so it didn't faze me.

When I'd finished, they told me that I had been very brave to come forward and that they would be visiting Bert that evening and would be in touch in due course to let me know what would happen next.

As we left the police station, I was overwhelmed with relief. No more secrets, no more lies. I was desperate for Bert to be punished. I just wished I could see his face when he opened the door to find the police on his doorstep. He deserved everything that happened to him now.

Over the next two weeks, I rushed home from school every day asking 'Have you heard anything yet?' I knew Bert would deny it all but I imagined we'd come face to face in a courtroom and I would stand and look him in the eye as I told everyone what he had done. He would break down and the judge would sentence him then and there. That was my fantasy. That's what I assumed would happen.

Auntie Vera rang me one day and she sounded odd on the phone. 'I'm sorry, Charlene, but you know I never suspected a thing. I never once saw anything untoward.'

'That's OK,' I said. I knew she hadn't known or she would have stopped him. Now I was a bit older, I understood that. I wondered why she felt she had to apologise, though. It's not as if it was her fault in any way.

Then one evening, about two weeks later, Paul Hilton came round to visit us. I was really pleased to see him at first but something about his expression made the smile fade from my face.

'The police have conducted extensive interviews with Bert,' he said, 'and as you probably expected he has denied it all.'

'Bastard!' Dad whispered.

'They have also interviewed other people who were in the house at the time – your aunt, your uncle, and your cousin Scott – but unfortunately, none of them can corroborate your statement. This means that it is his word against yours, and I'm afraid the Crown Prosecution Service have decided there is not enough evidence to take the case to court.'

'What does that mean?' I asked, stunned. 'What will happen to him?'

'Nothing, I'm afraid. There's nothing we can do without a witness.'

'But Penny said the police would believe me if I told the truth.'

'They do believe you,' he said. 'One hundred per cent. But they are not allowed to press charges without more evidence. I'm really sorry, Charlene.'

Dad had his face in his hands. I still didn't understand. 'He'll just go free without any punishment at all?'

'He's been told he's not allowed to come anywhere near you ever again, but he won't be punished as such.'

I jumped up, ran upstairs and flung myself on my bed, crying so hard I felt sick and giddy. Dad came up to try and comfort me but I couldn't stop howling for about two hours.

You bastard! I thought. After all that, you've got away with everything!

'He has to live with himself and what he's done,' Dad said, trying to calm me down.

But I didn't think he even felt as if he'd done anything wrong, and the police not pressing charges would back him up to his mind. He'd got away scot-free. He could go on and do it to some other girl in future, while I had to live with the knowledge that he was walking the streets of London, enjoying his life.

I was utterly distraught, and for several weeks I found it hard to get on with normal life. I was so angry I couldn't eat, sleep or think about anything else. The only thought in my head was that I wanted him to die and rot in hell.

18

Lisa

I was so proud of Charlene when she told the police about Bert. I knew how hard it had been for her, because she didn't want to upset her dad and her aunt and uncle – and anyway, it was difficult talking about these things. With Charlene, she likes to put her emotional problems in a box and lock them away, rather than making a song and dance about them, but the secret about Bert was eating away at her and it was much better to tell.

When she got the news that he wasn't being charged by the police, it was a huge slap in the face. She was literally floored by it. I've never seen her so upset or angry about anything. She said she didn't want to talk about it any more, but she became quite snappy after that, with other girls at school and sometimes with me. It's as though she was carrying the anger around with her and had to let it out somehow. She'd snap at me if I talked to anyone else at breaktime, or said I wasn't free to play with her after school, or even if she didn't like the colour of something I was wearing. It was a bit like walking on eggshells being around her at that time, but I knew it was all to do with Bert so I didn't mind.

I was walking on eggshells at home as well, because Dad was heartbroken. He was in mourning for Mum and because she wasn't there to take it out on, he was grumpy with us kids instead. If we made any noise at all, he would shout at us. The volume on the TV had to be turned down so low you could hardly hear it. Even my brother James was on best behaviour, but still Dad snapped at us, and it was especially difficult on Saturday mornings when we were getting ready to go and see Mum.

The arrangement was that at lunchtime on Saturday we went downstairs to my granddad's flat and Mum would pick us up from there to take us to the dingy little flat she shared with Tom.

The first time I met Tom, I couldn't for the life of me see how Mum could fancy him. He was fixing something in Granddad's car for him so I thought he must be a nice guy at least, but he looked disgusting to me. He was short with grey hair, his teeth were all brown as though he never brushed them and his breath smelt bad. I don't think he took a bath very often either. He had a thick Scottish accent so that half the time I couldn't understand what he was saying. But the worst thing was that as soon as we met him, he seemed to think he had to start being our surrogate father, laying down the law and telling us off about everything. We were getting enough of that at home and I didn't want to put up with it there as well from someone who wasn't even related to me.

'Isn't he lovely?' Mum giggled to me. 'I met him in a nightclub and fell for him straight away.'

I stared at her in amazement. How could she possibly

fall for someone like him? The only explanation was that my mother had never been very independent. She liked people to look after her: to mend things, pay the bills, fill out forms, cook the dinner. In some ways she was like a child. Maybe she thought Tom would take care of her. He had a kind of arrogance about him that might make you think he's a strong, capable kind of guy but I didn't fall for it. He might be good at fixing cars and doing odd jobs around the house, but I had a feeling that he wasn't as caring as Mum hoped, and I didn't think he was very smart either, from what I could make out.

'We're going to get married,' Mum confided. 'Just as soon as the divorce from your dad comes through. You and Christine will be my bridesmaids.'

I didn't want to be her bridesmaid. It felt disloyal to Dad to spend time with them, and as Tom got more controlling, I grew to dread the one day a week we went for a visit. He wanted to know everything about us. If James and I whispered something to each other, straight away Tom would be asking 'What did you say? What was it?' and pestering us until we told him.

Then one day, he followed me into the bedroom at their flat and sat down on the bed beside me. I felt instantly wary. What was he up to?

'You're so beautiful,' he said first, and reached out to stroke my face.

My skin prickled with fear. That was exactly what Alan had done, telling me I was beautiful and stroking my face. Was Tom going to try and have sex with me? I tried to pull away from his reach without being rude.

'It's OK,' he said, moving closer and still stroking my face. 'Did that man hurt you?'

'I don't want to talk about it,' I mumbled, and then I started crying. It was a dark, dingy bedroom, just as Alan's had been, and it was all coming back to me. I could feel the same fear and panic building inside me, and it felt horrible.

'Your mum's worried that you don't ever talk about it,' he said. 'She asked me to have a word.'

'I'm fine. Honestly.' I tried to move away along the bed, wiping my nose with the back of my hand. 'I'm just trying to forget about it all.'

He moved closer and I could smell his stale breath. 'You know where I am if you ever want to talk. I could maybe explain things to you a bit better because I'm a man and I understand other men.'

'OK,' I said. 'Can I go now? I need to get a tissue.'

He pulled a disgusting hanky out of his pocket and handed it to me, putting his arm around my shoulders. 'I think it would be better if you were able to talk about what happened,' he said. 'You can tell me anything you like. I won't be shocked.'

All I wanted was for him to let me go but I didn't think I could say that so I kept quiet.

'That man was an animal,' he said. 'You mustn't let it put you off other men you meet in future. We're not all like that.'

He was trying to sound all caring and concerned, but I knew he was being nosy. I could tell he wanted me to reveal the gory details and the thought made me feel sick.

While he went on talking about 'the way men are' and how he was different and only wanted to care for us children, all I could think about was how much I hated being so close to him and how much I wished he would let me go. I kept quiet until I couldn't bear it any longer. 'I need to go for a wee,' I said at last. Surely he couldn't argue with that.

'Just remember, Lisa,' he said, finally letting me go, 'any time you want to talk, you just say the word.'

I hurried out of the room and stormed through the flat looking for Mum. 'Did you ask Tom to talk to me about being kidnapped?' I asked her coldly.

'He suggested it and I thought it might help,' she said meekly. 'I thought maybe it would be easier to talk to him than your own family. After all, you've never wanted to talk about it with me or your dad.'

'You were bang out of order,' I told her. 'I don't like him and he's the last person I would ever talk to.'

Mum's face crumpled, as if she was going to cry. 'Why don't you like him? He's a lovely man.'

'He needs to stop poking his nose in my business,' I said. 'Look, Mum, don't tell him I said I don't like him. I'll try to get along with him but I just don't want to talk to him about personal things. OK?'

I should have guessed that Mum wouldn't be able to keep it to herself. That evening when I was drying dishes in the kitchen, Tom came in.

'Your mum says you don't like me,' he said in his broad accent. 'What's all that about?'

I gave a huge sigh. 'I'm sorry. I just didn't want to talk to you about the kidnapping, that's all.'

'We're pals, you and I,' he said, putting his arm around me and giving me a squeeze. 'Don't go saying stuff like that to your mum. She's in pieces about what happened to you so don't make it worse for her.'

I rubbed the plate I was drying furiously, thinking that if Mum had really been upset about what happened to me, maybe she shouldn't have left home a couple of weeks later. Maybe staying with her family would have been a better way of showing me how much she cared.

The following week when Dad took me to my counselling session I told Patricia about Tom sitting on the bed beside me telling me I was beautiful and how it reminded me of what Alan used to do. She and Dad were obviously horrified. I saw them glance at one another.

'That was a very difficult situation,' Patricia said carefully. 'But you handled it very well.'

Then she spoiled her nice words by saying, 'Why don't you draw a picture showing me how you felt about the event?'

I felt she was treating me like a baby with all her pictures, in which apparently the colours described my emotions, and her silly word games and card games. I'm not at nursery! I thought. It felt childish and patronising and I couldn't see that it was doing any good at all.

As the weeks passed, I begged Dad harder and harder to let me stop going. He had to bribe me with sweets to get me out of the door every time, and promise me treats afterwards as well.

'It's not doing any good,' I argued. 'Surely you can see that? It's just a complete waste of time.'

'The police recommended that you should do counselling, so we'd better do it for a while longer,' was his only argument.

'I just want to put the experience behind me. The counselling is stopping me from moving on,' I said. 'Besides, I hate going.'

But no matter how much I protested, I still forced to go along every week to see Patricia and play those stupid games.

At the end of May, we heard that Alan had been to court for his trial and had pleaded guilty to everything. Charlene told me about it because her dad had gone along to watch. She said the judge sentenced him to nine life sentences, which was fantastic news, even if I didn't quite understand it. Cats were supposed to have nine lives but not human beings.

Charlene explained: 'With one life sentence, you can sometimes get out for good behaviour, but with nine you never will.'

That was brilliant to hear. It meant we really could forget about him and get on with our lives. I brought it up with Dad before my counselling session the following week.

'It's time to move on now,' I told him. 'The court case is over. It's all history. I'm absolutely fine. I'm doing well at school, things are fine at home, I've got loads of friends and I'm not having the nightmares any more.' That last bit was a white lie but the rest was true. 'Can't I *please* stop going to see Patricia?'

'Alright then,' he said, smiling. 'I give in. You don't have to go any more.'

I flung my arms around him and gave him a big hug. 'Thanks, Dad. You're the best!'

Next day, as soon as I got to school, I ran up to tell Charlene.

She was a bit funny with me, because she hated her counselling as well. 'Why do you get to stop and I don't?'

'Ask your dad if you can stop,' I urged her. 'Tell him I've stopped now and he's bound to say yes. It's not fair that you have to do it if I don't.'

The following day she came to school in an absolutely foul mood. 'They obviously think I'm madder than you,' she told me, 'Because Dad says I have to keep going.'

'Oh no!' I was genuinely sympathetic. 'How can he do that?'

'Probably because you're Miss Goody Two-shoes, always doing your schoolwork on time and never back-chatting anyone. People like you make it harder for the rest of us, you know.'

I was stunned and looked at her to see if she was joking but she didn't appear to be.

'You got to have your dad sitting in with you so you never did proper counselling anyway,' she said. 'It doesn't even count.'

'Yes, it does. I hated it. She treated me like a baby.'

'You are a baby,' she said. 'A crybaby. You just turn on the waterworks every time so people see you expressing your "feelings" and they don't worry about you any more. I don't burst into tears at the drop of a hat so I have to keep doing counselling so they can try and force me to have more "feelings."' She sounded really angry with me now.

'Look, I know it's not fair,' I said, 'but it's not my fault. I didn't make the decision.'

'Yeah, right,' she said. 'Just get out of my face, Lisa Hoodless.'

She turned and walked off, leaving me staring open-mouthed. We'd never had a falling out like that before and I didn't know how to react. Should I run after her and try to make things up straight away? Or let her cool down and call her later? I could understand why she was upset but I couldn't bear it if we fell out over it. I needed her. We'd said we'd be friends for ever. We had to be.

19

Charlene

Dad went to Alan Hopkinson's trial, on 28 May 1999. I was curious about it but he wouldn't tell me much.

'It didn't last very long because he pleaded guilty. That's the main thing. And he's gone to jail for life,' he said.

'What did you think of him?' I asked, curious.

'To be honest? Nothing. I thought he was a total nothing, really. You can't tell anything just by looking at people.'

'Did he look upset?' I asked.

'He just kept his head down. He didn't look up at anyone, not even the judge. He's got an illness that can't be cured and now they're going to lock him up and throw away the key. So that's a result.'

He wouldn't say any more, so I left it at that. The next morning, though, when we were in Tesco, I saw Alan's picture on the front page of a newspaper. The headline read: 'Jailed. Nine life sentences.' It felt funny seeing his face there. I started to read the story underneath but Lisa and I weren't mentioned in it. It just said he'd been jailed for sexual offences against young girls.

Nine lives sounded like an impossibly long time. If a life is about seventy years, then nine lives would be about six hundred and thirty years.

'They run concurrently,' Dad explained briefly. 'At the same time.'

I still didn't understand but that sounded like a proper punishment for what Alan had done, so I put it out of my mind.

Then Lisa told me she was stopping her counselling. That night I had a huge argument with Dad.

'She hasn't had as tough a life as you,' he explained. 'You've got a lot more to deal with, what with your mum dying and then Bert.' He spat the name out. I could tell he hated even thinking about him.

'She's had to deal with her mum leaving,' I pleaded. 'We've both dealt with our stuff and moved on. Dad, please let me stop.'

He shook his head. 'You can't say I'm not indulging you in every other way, but you have to bear with me on this. I don't know why Lisa's dad let her stop, but I think it's doing you some good and I think you've still got some issues to work through.'

He had started going to counselling himself, and since then he kept coming out with meaningless and infuriating phrases like 'issues to work through'. I didn't usually backchat Dad but I was very upset that Lisa had been allowed to stop and I hadn't.

'You're the one who needs counselling, not me,' I yelled. 'You're just trying to make yourself feel better, but it's making me feel worse! It's making me really depressed.'

'You have to talk to Penny about that next time,' he said calmly, making me even madder.

'You don't know anything about how I feel or you wouldn't be doing this! You don't care that it makes me miserable because every time I have to remember what happened all over again. It's almost as though you're punishing me for being abducted.'

'I'm sorry, but you're not going to shift me on this one, sweetie. I'll get you new clothes if you want them, I'll get you sweets, or take you to the cinema, whatever you want, but I think it's important you keep going to counselling.'

I stormed out of the room, slamming the door as hard as I could, absolutely furious with him. Why could he not understand how I felt? Why was he being so mean?

Next day when I saw Lisa smiling away in the playground I transferred all my anger onto her instead. How come she was allowed to be happy again? I hated her for being cheerful and for getting over things, while I was forced to stay back in that 'invalid' state with everyone tiptoeing round me. And I decided that it was all because I had had a worse time with Alan, and my poisonous thoughts about how it was Lisa's fault we were kidnapped came back to me. She'd got off lightly. She owed me for going along to look after her. Instead, I felt as though she had left me behind.

I found it hard to be nice to Lisa for a while. I was very snappy with her sometimes, but she never seemed to hold it against me. I didn't tell her but I felt as though I had been betrayed by her. It was as if she had let me down.

'Do you still have those nightmares about Alan?' I asked one day.

'Yeah,' she admitted. 'I keep my piggy lamp on so I can see when I wake up. It's not every night, but quite often.'

I hadn't had a single nightmare about being at Alan's. Not one. I had dreams about Bert sometimes, but not Alan. From the minute I got back I could sleep in the dark without a problem. In fact, I prefer pitch dark – I don't like sleeping with the light on. So didn't that mean I was recovering faster than Lisa?

I didn't want to go out on my own, but we weren't allowed to anyway. Philomena or Dad would take me to school and pick me up again, and if I was going shopping or to a friend's they always dropped me off at the front door. Lisa was the same, though. I couldn't imagine why people would think she was getting over things more quickly than I was. She was just the same as me. We were both fine as long as people left us alone to live our normal lives.

I started to make a new group of friends in Year Seven – Stacey and Cheryl especially – and by the end of the year I knew I was Miss Popular. I became very cocky and bigheaded because everyone was my friend. They were all fascinated that I had been kidnapped by a paedophile and wanted to know about it. I thrived on being the centre of attention and gradually Lisa and I drifted further and further apart.

She was quieter, more of a good girl in class and not very pushy, whereas I became mouthy and confident. I wasn't naughty in school but I could be stroppy and cheeky behind the teachers' backs. Lisa started hanging out with the geeky set that got the good marks in everything, while I never did my homework. The gap between us was widening. In fact, part of the reason I was failing most exams was that I was dyslexic but at the time I just thought that studying wasn't cool and I preferred hanging out with my mates.

I still felt angry when I looked at Lisa. I couldn't help thinking that the kidnapping was all her fault. I'd gone along to look after her when I could have saved myself, and after we were rescued she just dumped me and went off with her other friends. It wasn't rational but that was how I felt.

Gradually Stacey became my best friend. She was incredibly pretty, with long, light brown hair, and she dressed really nicely. She wanted to be a hairdresser and would try out lots of different styles on me: plaiting my hair, pinning it up, curling it. I think it was her who first started taking the piss out of Lisa's hair, which was quite frizzy, wiry hair that looked dry and damaged. She was also much shorter than the rest of us in the class, and one day I coined a nickname for her – Matted Mini-me. Somehow it stuck and we all started calling her Matted Mini-me whenever we passed her in the corridor or the playground. It wasn't that funny, but everyone picked up on it.

One day, as my little gang passed Lisa in the playground, I said nastily, 'Oh, there's Matted Mini-me' and she turned to look at me with such a hurt, accusing expression that I felt terrible. But then straight afterwards it made me feel even angrier. She had no right to complain about a few names after what she had done to me. It got to the stage where I couldn't bear to be in the same room as her because of the uncomfortable emotions it stirred up: anger, hatred, guilt and a deep sadness for the loss of the person with whom I'd sworn to be friends for life.

Lisa never said anything to me about it. She never asked why I was being mean, never tried to fight back in any way. I almost wished she had come up and confronted me because then I could have yelled some of the things that were on my mind and eating away at me. Maybe a big screaming argument would have done us a lot of good; but on the other hand, perhaps it could have turned nasty and made things even worse. The fact was that Lisa's passiveness in the face of the insults made me feel even more determined to hurt her.

In September 2000 we started at Filsham Secondary School and once again Lisa was in my class. My bullying campaign notched up a gear and I started manipulating situations and spreading lies to try to make everyone else in the class hate Lisa as much as I did.

'I heard Lisa calling you a slag,' I told one girl. 'She said your boyfriend is only going out with you because you're so easy.'

The girl in question charged up to Lisa, yelling in her face. 'Why are you saying stuff about me behind my back?'

Lisa would defend herself quietly. 'I'm not, really. I didn't say that.'

But they believed me, and Lisa's treatment got worse.

Stacey used to sit behind her in class and pretend to whisper and then laugh, so that Lisa thought she was whispering about her. If we walked into the toilet and Lisa was there, we would hold our noses and say 'Ugh!' and walk out again. Every time I got a new recruit into the 'I hate Lisa' campaign, I felt triumphant. Stacey and I were the class leaders, the most popular girls that everyone wanted to hang out with, so they didn't get friendly with Lisa if they knew what was good for them. If you were a friend of hers, you were no friend of ours.

Once or twice Dad asked me why we never saw Lisa around the house any more.

I wrinkled up my nose. 'She's become really stuck-up. She thinks she's the greatest,' I said.

'That doesn't sound like her,' he said, giving me an enquiring look. 'Why don't you make more effort? Ask her over for tea at the weekend.'

'Nah. She'll be hanging out with her geeky friends all doing their homework,' I sneered.

'And that's bad, is it?' he asked with a raised eyebrow.

He finally let me stop going to counselling in October 2000 after a year and a half of weekly sessions with Penny. I still felt furious that I'd had to go for so much longer than Lisa. I was mostly angry with her, but I was angry with Dad as well. What with that and my teenage hormones kicking in, I was a bit of a nightmare at home.

When I was twelve Dad split up with Philomena and I think I was at least partly the reason. I'd often heard them arguing about me because she thought Dad was spoiling me after I got kidnapped by doing whatever I wanted, buying me whatever I asked for and letting me get away with being cheeky to her. She started trying to tell me off about things and I got more and more rude back and Dad always took my side.

When she finally left, I was glad to see the back of her. It was just Dad and me now and that's the way I wanted it. I had to do all the cooking and cleaning round the place and became the lady of the house. No one could tell me what to do: not Penny, or Philomena, or Dad, or my teachers. All I cared about was hanging out with my friends and being one of the most popular girls in the school.

20

Lisa

Towards the end of Year Six and over that summer of 1999, Charlene was getting tetchy with me quite a lot, as though I irritated her, but she never said why. I assumed it was because she was upset about Bert not being charged, and the fact she still had to do counselling while I didn't, so I tried to be as nice as possible. But in Year Seven, things went from bad to worse. Charlene made it clear that she didn't want to be my friend any more. Now when I looked at her, I saw anger and dislike in her eyes though I had no idea what I'd done to make her hate me. Then she came up with the hurtful nickname 'Matted Mini-me'. I'd always had really curly hair and I used to wash it and let it dry naturally, which I suppose made it a bit frizzy and that's why the name-calling started. I had buck teeth as well, and although I was tiny my bum was quite big and out of proportion, so I got teased about all these things. Toothy, frizzy, big bum: why was I so ugly?

Once we started at Filsham Secondary School it got much worse. Lots of different people joined in but it broke my heart that Charlene was involved. What had made her turn against me like this, and start to bully me so badly? I wished I could talk to her and find out what I'd done to deserve it, but I didn't have the courage to approach her. She looked at me with contempt sometimes as if I was some disgusting substance she'd scraped off her shoe. I used to run home after school and lock myself in my bedroom crying my eyes out about it, but there was no one I could tell. I wouldn't have confided in Christine or James, and Dad was still depressed about Mum leaving so I couldn't bother him. It didn't occur to me to tell a teacher; that would have been too embarrassing, and it might have made things worse anyway.

At first I thought it was my own fault I was being bullied: I'd tug and tug at my hair with a comb after washing to try and make it sit flat, but I didn't have any straighteners in those days so it would spring straight back out as it dried. When people came up to me and accused me of saying things I hadn't said, I'd be all meek and apologetic and I hated myself for it. Why didn't I have the courage to fight back? Why didn't I stand up for myself? No wonder they bullied me when I was such a doormat.

I was terrified of Stacey, Charlene's new best friend. She was very popular but you wouldn't want to get on the wrong side of her, and if she came up to abuse me about something I would just mumble and slink away as soon as I could. I would never have said anything rude about Stacey. I wouldn't have dared.

Then there was a girl called Kim, who would be my friend one day and the next she would pick on me. I never knew what to expect. There were a lot of craneflies in that school and Kim knew I hated them, so she would collect a load of them – ten or twenty – and stuff them in my schoolbag. I was such a wimp that I would scream, drop the bag and run away and I'd have to get someone else to empty them out for me before I'd go near it again.

Kim and I did Food Technology together and she was always throwing flour at me when the teacher wasn't looking, but then the next day she would want to be friends again and I would be pathetically grateful. It's just horrible being bullied. It affects your whole self-image and all you want is for the bullies to change their minds and like you. You don't have the confidence to walk away – or at least I didn't, at that stage.

I wasn't even safe when I got home from school because sometimes a group of girls would ring me in the evenings.

'Do you fancy Kim's boyfriend?' someone would ask.

'No,' I'd say.

'She says she does,' I'd hear them call out, and I knew I'd be in for trouble with Kim at school the next day. There was no respite.

There always seemed to be stories circulating about things I was supposed to have said or done, and some were more hurtful than others. But the worst was when I heard that Charlene had supposedly said that when we were in the flat with Alan, I was enjoying it. The rumour spread round the school that I hadn't been screaming in pain but in pleasure. According to them, I loved having sex with him. When I heard that, I felt physically sick. I went to the toilets and locked myself in a cubicle right through lunchtime, bent double, tears streaming down my face. I didn't know if Charlene had really said that, but if she had it seemed like the ultimate betrayal after everything we had been through together. It seemed like the final nail in the coffin of our friendship. How could we ever be close again after that?

When I asked around, I finally found it hadn't been Charlene after all but I was still really upset about it.

Fortunately, I had a couple of other friends. I was close to two girls – Sam and Amie, who were very nice and sweet. I'd look at them sometimes and wonder why I got bullied and they didn't. Like me, Amie was a good girl who did her homework and didn't cheek the teachers, so why did no one pick on her? Or Sam? But neither of them had frizzy hair, and they didn't say stupid things the way I sometimes did. And Charlene didn't hate them. That was the root of the problem.

I sat in my room at home in the evenings, going over and over my relationship with Charlene, looking for clues about what I had done wrong. Maybe she didn't like it that I'd seen her being so vulnerable in the flat with Alan. I'd been the one who argued with him more while she just put up with it. I remembered the expression on her face when I walked in on them that evening at Alan's parents' place, when she was on her hands and knees: she'd been humiliated and upset that I saw her like that. Then I remembered something she'd said once, that it was me Alan was following, not her. Did she think it was my fault we'd been kidnapped? But that wasn't fair. No matter how much I looked at it, I couldn't see that I'd done anything bad to her. I'd only ever tried to be her best friend.

So it must just be because I wasn't a cool person. I didn't have the right shoes or the right schoolbag. My dad had left work because he had baby Georgie to look after and he'd gone on benefits to support the four of us. It was a struggle for him, so I didn't get new clothes very often. When we started secondary school I didn't have the proper Filsham jumper and I had to wear the same clothes over and over again until they were completely worn out. Meanwhile, Charlene had bang-up-to-date outfits because there was only her to buy for and her dad absolutely doted on her. I couldn't compete with that.

One of the last times Charlene was friendly to me was when Mum and Tom were getting married, in spring 2000. I had nothing to wear and no money to buy anything new, so Charlene lent me her lovely brown fitted jacket with leopard fur round the collar. It was a gorgeous jacket, and it was very sweet of her to offer it. I think she knew how much I was dreading the day. I still looked terrible, though, because I had nothing to wear with Charlene's jacket except a black skirt and my black school shoes with white socks. I had an argument with my dad because I wanted to wear the socks rolled down over my shoes, trainer-style, but he insisted I had to pull them up to my knees. I look like a complete idiot in the photos.

The wedding was in a registry office, with a reception in a pub afterwards, and I just felt horrible all day for my dad's sake. I pictured him sitting at home on his own while the woman he still loved was celebrating her new love, and I wished I hadn't gone. I'd rather have been sitting at home with him, keeping him company. I know he still minded about Mum and Tom. It used to wind him up when they came round to visit Granddad downstairs. They'd be trooping in and out and you could hear their voices and Mum's peals of laughter and Dad would have a face like thunder. If we were playing in the front garden when they came over during the week, Dad would call us all to come inside. I'd often go down to Granddad's in the evenings so he could help with my homework, but Dad would make me come back upstairs if Mum and Tom turned up.

A few months after the wedding, Dad announced that we were moving. He didn't say why but I knew it was so that he didn't have to see Mum and Tom together any more. The new place wasn't far – just a few streets away – but I was sad that I wouldn't be upstairs from Granddad any more. The day we moved in, I had to help Dad with unpacking everything, putting bedding on the beds, finding the kettle to make a cup of tea, heating spaghetti on toast for supper and generally being the 'mum' of the household. Dad seemed to be leaning on me more and more as I grew up, so I had that pressure at home, and the bullying at school, and weekends with Mum and the dreaded Tom. My life was pretty miserable all through that period.

Granddad was heartbroken when we moved. I promised I'd still be popping in all the time to see him, but obviously it wasn't as often as when we had lived upstairs. Life got too busy, helping Dad to run the new house, so I was probably only seeing him once or twice during the week instead of every day. Mum and Tom moved into our old place upstairs, so when I was there for the weekend I saw Granddad then. I still went to ask for his help when I had tricky homework to do and he still brought me chocolate digestive biscuits, on a plate to catch the crumbs.

Then Granddad's health began to fail. He had a stroke and heart problems and when I was fourteen, he died. The pain was unbearable. No one close to me had ever died before and I just couldn't accept it. I sank into a deep depression, just crawling through day-to-day life, feeling as though everything was meaningless. Getting up in the morning was a struggle. I hated my life and what it had become.

One evening just after this, Kim rang up and yelled down the phone at me over a stupid argument about who was going to Party in the Park with her. I'd said I would go with Sam, but Kim claimed I was betraying her. After our fight, I knew that the bullying at school would get worse and I couldn't handle it. I just broke down and sobbed.

I came off the phone and ran outside to sit in the swing in our back garden, crying my eyes out. Before long, the back door opened and Dad came out.

'What's up?' he asked, putting his arm around me. 'Who's upset you?'

'It's Kim,' I stammered. 'She says she won't be my friend any more.'

'But you've got lots of other friends,' he reasoned. 'You can afford to let one go if she's not being nice to you.'

'I haven't got lots of friends, Dad. Most people at school hate me.'

I blurted out about them calling me Matted Mini-me, and making up stories about me and holding their noses when I walked past. There was even a girl who had punched me once.

'How long has this been going on?' he asked quietly.

'Since Year Seven.'

'That long? Why didn't you tell someone before now? Why didn't you tell *me*, Lisa?'

'You've been so sad about Mum. I didn't want to make it worse.'

'Oh, Lisa, Lisa.' There was a long pause. 'I've let you down and I'm sorry. What are we going to do about this? Would you like me to talk to your teacher?'

'No!' I said quickly. 'That would only make things worse.'

'Well, why don't we find out about moving you to another school? There are plenty of places you could go. How about Claverham?'

I thought about that for a minute and it sounded like a good idea. Not having to face Charlene, Stacey and Kim every morning would be a huge weight off my mind. 'OK,' I sniffed. 'When would I be able to move?'

'I'll find out,' he said, 'but probably at the start of next term. Do you think you can wait? It's only a few weeks to go.'

'Yeah. I can wait.'

He went and got the forms from Claverham the very next day and we filled them in together, but at the last minute I changed my mind. If I could just get through one more year at Filsham, then I could go on to a sixth-form college and leave all this behind. It didn't seem worthwhile moving for the sake of one year.

And, funnily enough, once I'd made this decision, things got a bit easier at school anyway. I don't think it's because I was standing up for myself any more than I had before but the other girls seemed to be less interested in tormenting me. They probably had other things on their minds. I just kept my head down and passed my exams and stayed out of the way of trouble as much as I could.

21

Charlene

I wasn't a normal teenager, in that I never liked going out to nightclubs and pubs. I hated drinking and didn't enjoy being around people who drank, so that was part of it. I felt more comfortable having my friends round to my place or going to someone else's house; I still didn't like going out on my own. Obviously I had to go out sometimes during the day, maybe just popping out for a magazine or to post a letter, but I'd never go out on my own at night. I'd always make sure there was someone around to walk me home or I'd ask Dad to come and collect me. I'd look into the shadows and imagine something evil in there, or freak myself out thinking I could hear funny noises. Maybe it was a side-effect of having been kidnapped – I suppose it was – but at the same time lots of girls feel nervous about going out at night. It's a dangerous world out there.

I had a couple of short-term boyfriends when I was fifteen. They were nothing serious, but one of them was three years older and he introduced me to ecstasy pills. I was nervous about taking them at first because I'd read in the papers about how you can die when you take the very first one, and I'd always said I would never do drugs because of my mum. But after I started, I liked the way they made me feel relaxed and chatty, so I could just sit and talk all night without ever running out of things to say. Even better, after a few weeks of taking pills every weekend, my weight went right down from a size twelve to a size eight, and I loved being skinny. You can't eat when you take pills or you're sick, and you don't feel hungry at all.

At first I could take one pill and be off my face for half the night, but as I took more and more, sometimes I'd have to double-drop to get the same effect. Then I'd take two and I'd need another one half an hour later just to get the same sort of buzz. I couldn't really do much except chat when I'd taken them – I certainly couldn't get up and make a cup of tea or anything – so I was careful not to take pills at home. Dad would have gone berserk, with his drug-addiction history. He had no idea I was taking anything. He commented on my weight loss a couple of times, or wondered why I'd made a roast dinner on a Sunday but didn't feel like eating any of it, but I'm convinced he never once suspected about the pills.

I would have stopped taking them long before I did, but I didn't want to put the weight back on again. I started smoking cigarettes around this time, which Dad was disappointed about but he couldn't say anything because he smoked as well.

And then, just before my sixteenth birthday, I met a boy called Dean. He had a reputation for being 'hard', but when he rode up to our school playing field on a moped and asked me out, I was flattered and excited. He wasn't particularly good-looking but I thought I would be safe going out with someone like him – no one was going to come up and make trouble because of his reputation. Straight away I said, 'Yes, OK, I'll go out with you.'

We got close very quickly, and confided in each other about our pasts. I told him about being abused by Bert and abducted by Alan, and he was lovely about it and said he would never let anyone hurt me again. When I finally plucked up the courage to have sex with him, he was gentle and patient and made me feel absolutely fine about it. Sometimes I got flashbacks but I just told him about them and he stopped doing whatever it was and held me close.

As I found out more about Dean, I realised he desperately needed someone to look after him. He often went days without eating a proper meal, so I would bring him food and cook for him. He shared a house with his two brothers, which was dirty, messy and had hardly any furniture. I bought paint and painted his bedroom, I bought new bedding for his bed and curtains for his windows, and I cleaned up the whole house and brought in supplies. My dad gave me a very generous allowance so I was always giving Dean money for fags and booze and whatever else he wanted, but I didn't feel I was being taken advantage of because I loved him – and I thought it was mutual. I was falling in love and started having fantasies about marrying him and spending the rest of my life with him.

The changes happened gradually after we'd been

together about eight months. When he'd been drinking he would become critical and nasty. I'd stopped taking ecstasy because Dean didn't approve of drugs and as a consequence I'd put on a bit of weight, and he told me I was getting fat. He'd say he didn't like what I was wearing, or that I was ugly – but only when he was drunk, so I blamed the booze, not him. He didn't even know what he was saying when he was plastered. I tried to stop him going out boozing so often but then I was accused of trying to split him up from his mates, and he'd say it was boring spending time with me on my own.

I got more and more depressed and determined to win back his love by being the perfect girlfriend. I'd never pester him but I'd wait in until he called and said he wanted to see me. I'd buy him whatever he asked for. I'd be his doormat, basically.

And then, when we'd been going out for about a year, he was arrested for stabbing someone. He was sentenced to twenty months in jail, of which he served ten. I should have broken up with him then and there, but I didn't. Instead, I turned up at the prison every two weeks to visit, and I sent him money so he could buy fags and stamps. I'd never get any praise for what I was doing, though – only abuse. He was constantly accusing me of being unfaithful to him. Seemingly his friends told him they'd seen me with someone else, which was nonsense, but he believed them instead of believing me. His mates were obviously just stirring things up for a laugh, but stuck in jail Dean got really paranoid about it and gave me all sorts of grief.

My dad hated him by this stage and kept trying to talk me into leaving him because he could see how horrible Dean was being and how miserable it was making me. 'You deserve much better,' he said. 'Have more self-respect, Char. He's no good.'

All my friends were telling me the same thing: that I should leave him and that I shouldn't put up with his behaviour, but I'd got it into my head that Dean was the boy for me. He was my first love and I wanted to stick by him. No matter how bad it got, I kept trying to please him and make him love me back, the way he had loved me in the beginning.

Once he got out of jail, things went from bad to worse. Nothing I could do was right. He'd disappear for days on end and refuse to tell me where he'd been. He told me I would never be able to get another boyfriend because no one else would ever put up with me. He made me feel so low that I believed all the abusive things he said. It got so bad that if he went out for five minutes, I'd be having panic attacks, worrying about whether he was with another girl. I felt as though I couldn't breathe if I didn't know exactly where he was and who he was with. He told me I was worthless and stupid and paranoid and I believed him. My confidence hit rock bottom. From dawn to dusk, I couldn't stop myself from worrying about what he was up to when we weren't together.

One day he left his phone behind and I opened it to read through his old texts. All my suspicions were confirmed when I found one from a girl I knew that said, 'Your sex is good. Do you regret fucking me?'

It was a complete slap in the face. It couldn't have been more blatant but when I confronted him about it, he denied that anything had happened and called me a 'fucking psycho'. Then he came home with a lovebite on his neck and still he said he wasn't being unfaithful to me. His sister Kasey, who's a friend of mine, caught him in bed with another girl and called to tell me but he always had an excuse for everything. It was my fault, because I was so possessive and paranoid. Even when a girl confessed to me that she was sleeping with Dean, he wouldn't admit it. It was all in my head, he said.

By this stage, I got a sick feeling in my stomach whenever I was with him, but still I couldn't let him go. He dragged me down so low that I couldn't function any more, couldn't find the courage or the energy to break away. In the end I was with him for three and a half years before I finally managed to make the break – and even then I hoped for a while that we'd get back together. I always thought I could make things better again. I just wanted to get back to how it had been in the first eight months when we fell in love, before it all went wrong.

Now, I can look back and see that I was with Dean for all the wrong reasons. I wanted to feel safe. I wanted to feel needed. I liked cooking and cleaning and looking after him. I didn't recognise that I was being abused again – in a different way from the way Bert and Alan had abused me, but it was abuse all the same. In order to heal I had to learn to listen to all the good people around about me and start looking after myself instead of trying to find someone else to protect me. I needed to develop more self-esteem so that I didn't let anyone walk all over me. It was a lesson it took me a long time to learn, and one that I had to learn the hard way.

22

Lisa

During my last year at Filsham, I worked hard and got six GCSEs with good grades, then in May 2005, straight after finishing my exams, I walked out of that school for the last time, and away from the group of girls who had made my life so miserable. I applied and was accepted to study catering at Hastings College, starting the following September, and then Nan came to me with an offer I couldn't refuse. She had been invited out to Australia to visit some old friends of hers but she was nervous about making the trip on her own. Would I come with her, all expenses paid? We'd be away for five weeks altogether and no one else could spare the time.

I was over the moon. Until then, I had never even been out of the country and all of a sudden I was booking a plane ticket to the other side of the world. I'd fancied going to Australia ever since Tracey Christmas told me about it. It was the best thing that had ever happened to me at that point and I was buzzing with excitement as I bought all the things I needed and got my suitcase ready.

A couple of weeks before I left, my friend Sam took me round to visit a friend of hers and he had a visitor sitting at his kitchen table, a guy called Tony. Tony was very tall, with dark curly hair, and he had his arm in a sling after an accident in which he was trimming a hedge with a hedge trimmer that slipped and cut through a nerve in his little finger. We got chatting and I liked him straight away but I didn't think for a minute that he'd be interested in me. I thought he was attractive, while I was Matted Mini-me. He was twenty-two and I was only sixteen. He had a job and a car, while I hadn't even started college.

Later that night I nearly jumped out of my skin with excitement when I got a text from Tony saying, 'Hi, how you doing? I thought you were looking really nice today.' He asked if I wanted to go to the beach with him the following day and I was so chuffed I could hardly sleep that night. I got up early and spent ages getting ready in my best skirt, with perfect make-up and freshly washed and straightened hair. If he only knew how long I spent getting ready to meet him just to wander round the seafront arcades he'd have thought I was mad!

We had a great day out, playing the fruit machines, going for a walk on the pier and messing around, then we went to a pub for a few drinks in the evening. When he dropped me back home, we had a kiss and a cuddle in the car. I'd already told him that I was going to Australia for five weeks. I was worried that might put him off, but he said, 'I really like you, Lisa. I'll wait for you while you're away because I want us to be together.'

It was an amazing feeling for me, realising that someone liked me for who I was. He thought I was pretty and sweet and he enjoyed spending time with me. He obviously hadn't heard that I'd been kidnapped when I was ten – he wasn't one of our crowd from school so there was no reason why he'd have associated me with that old news story. I didn't tell him at that stage because I thought it might scare him away, but he said he was ready to wait until I felt comfortable before we had sex.

I went off to Australia and had a magical holiday out there. We were staying most of the time with some elderly relatives of Nan's near Brisbane, but they had a swimming pool and a big patio where we had barbecues in the evening. Even though it was their winter, the weather was gorgeous and I spent a lot of time working on getting a good tan. We travelled down to New South Wales after that and my favourite thing was when we went out whale-watching in the ocean. We sailed far out till you couldn't see the land any more, and suddenly the boat was surrounded by dolphins leaping and playing in the water. On the horizon we could see some whales, their big tails splashing down on the surface and water puffing out of their blowholes. I was mesmerised and wanted to stay out there all day, the sight was so incredible.

All in all, it was a trip of a lifetime, made even more special because I had a wonderful man waiting for me back in Hastings. I spent idle moments just lying around daydreaming about him and imagining what it would be like when I got back. I called him twice and both times he said he missed me and couldn't wait to see me.

When I got home, I just fell into his arms. We became inseparable. I started my college course but he would pick me up at five after his work and we'd see each other every evening, then at weekends I'd go over to stay in his flat. When we had sex, it was fantastic and I had no problems at all with memories of Alan. That all seemed so long ago, in another lifetime. I eventually told Tony about it and he was very sweet and caring, but to be honest it didn't affect me any more.

The first time Dad saw me sitting in the car with Tony outside our house, he went mad. It was obvious that Tony was much older than me and Dad suspected that he would be up to no good hanging around with a young girl. I had to cross my fingers and promise that he was just a good friend or I could have been facing a curfew. I'm not sure if Dad believed me, but at least we were able to continue seeing each other. I think if anyone had tried to stop us, I'd have run away from home. I was head over heels in love.

And then, when we'd been sleeping together for less than a month, I discovered that I was pregnant. We went to the doctor together for me to have a test and before he told us the result, the doctor asked, 'What do you want it to be? Positive or negative?'

We both said 'Positive!' at the same time. We were still in our honeymoon period and so loved-up that having our own baby seemed perfect even though I was so young – only just seventeen.

Of course, it wasn't perfect because it was going to mess up my college course and the career in catering I had planned. I worked out the dates and decided I would finish my first year of college and sit the exams to get the

Level One qualification, then I'd have to take time out for a couple of years to look after the baby. Tony reassured me that we would get a little place together and we'd be a perfect happy family. He took an evening job working in a bar to try and save money and I felt reassured that he would look after us.

The next problem was how to tell my dad. I was quaking in my boots worrying about what his reaction would be. To him I was still just a little girl. I delayed breaking the news until I was about four months pregnant and starting to show. Tony offered to come and talk to Dad with me, but I said it was best coming from me on my own.

I waited till all the others had gone to bed one night then I went in to the front room where Dad was sitting watching TV.

'Dad, I need to talk to you,' I said. He put his paper down and looked up and I froze. The words just wouldn't come out.

'What is it?' he asked.

Suddenly I just blurted it out in a rush. 'I'm pregnant, and I'm having the baby.'

There was a long pause when he sat staring at me without speaking. The tension was unbearable. Finally he said, 'You know what's going to happen, don't you? You're going to be stuck living on benefits for the next eighteen years, just like me. Do you think that's a fun life?'

'My boyfriend Tony is going to support us,' I said. 'He's saving up to get us a place.'

'Is he that older guy I saw you with?'

I nodded.

'He should be ashamed of himself, wrecking a young girl's life like that. When is he getting this place, then?'

'We're planning to move in together as soon as the baby is born,' I said. 'It's due next June.'

'Good!' he said. 'Because you're not living here when that baby's born. I am not raising any more children.'

'Fair enough,' I said. I didn't mention that it was his first grandchild we were talking about. I'd been planning to move out anyway, so that didn't matter.

It was very painful that my father couldn't be happy for me at all, when I was so sure that it was going to be alright. What hurt the most was that Dad stopped talking to me from that day onwards. We'd been much closer since Mum had left and I'd had to take on so much of the responsibility for looking after us all but now it seemed that was all finished. We lived under the same roof for another five months, but he never said anything to me except passing comments about domestic arrangements like when he was doing a laundry or what time dinner would be ready. He never asked if I was feeling alright or how I was getting on at college or anything like that. It got to the stage where if he was in the front room I wouldn't dare go in there. I stayed out of his way as much as I could.

It's not that he was a mean person; he was just deeply disappointed in me. James and Christine were both rebels but I was the good daughter, the one who worked hard and did well at school, and he'd had high hopes for me. As far as he was concerned, I blew all those hopes sky-high as soon as I got pregnant. I would never amount to anything now in his opinion.

By contrast, Mum was delighted when I told her, and looking forward to playing with her little grandchild. She had stopped being like a parent to me. She tried to be my mate rather than my mum, but to be frank I would rather have had a mum.

Still, at least I had Tony and I thought that was all going well until one evening, when I was about six months pregnant, he threw a wobbly. I think it was just starting to dawn on him that he wasn't going to be able to go out with his mates and lead the carefree lifestyle he was used to once the baby was born and we were living together. I don't know why he hadn't thought it through before – I certainly had and I was six years younger than him.

'I'm just not sure I want to be with you any more,' he said, to my horror.

I could hardly believe what I was hearing. How had things changed so quickly? A few months before we were going to be the perfect family, and now he wanted to leave me before our child was even born? I exploded. 'I'm going to be homeless in three months because my dad's kicking me out. What am I supposed to do? Be a single mother at seventeen? I had everything going for me before you came along – my place at college, a career to follow. You've ruined my life!'

'It's just that you're so young and immature. I'm going to have to take all the responsibility,' he said.

'I'm sorry, but it's too late to think of that now. What's

done is done!' I was furious but I was also desperately upset because I was still madly in love with him. I couldn't bear to let him go. What on earth would I do without him?

We made up a few days later, but something had changed in the relationship. He seemed to resent me, as if it was my fault that I'd got pregnant, not his. He started bossing me around – for example, calling me at college to tell me to come home and make him a sausage baguette – and I just obeyed because I was terrified of losing him and didn't want any conflict. It wasn't an ideal situation to bring a young child into, but I still hoped that when the baby was born Tony would fall in love with it and all our dreams of being a happy family would work out after all. I wanted the fairytale ending – the kind that never happens in real life.

I needed my girlfriends to get me through that difficult time, and Sam and Amie were just brilliant. They were there whenever I needed to talk about things, or just lie on their sofas and sob. And then, in a quite extraordinary turn of events, I found there was one other person who was on my side, who I could rely on when it mattered.

One evening while I was still staying at my dad's, the telephone rang. Dad called out that it was for me so I picked it up and was startled to hear Charlene's voice on the end of the line.

'Hi, how are you?' she said.

'OK,' I said cautiously, listening to see if I could hear other girls giggling in the background. I thought she must be ringing to cause trouble and I was wondering, Oh my

God, what have I done now? Whose boyfriend are they going to accuse me of fancying?

'Have you heard about Daniel?' she asked.

A boy called Daniel whom we had both known at primary school had just died in a car accident on the Battle Road, with four other people in the car. 'Yeah, it's really sad, isn't it?' I said. I knew Charlene had been very close to him.

Then she said in a quiet voice, 'I'm really sorry, Lisa.'

'What for?'

'I'm sorry for being so horrible to you. You should have been the one person I could talk to all these years and instead I was awful to you. It was only when Dan died that I started thinking about who my true friends really are, and I realised you are definitely one of them.'

I was so surprised, I couldn't think what to say, so I just said 'Thanks.' I still suspected it might be a trick of some kind.

'I'm having a really hard time just now,' she continued. 'Things aren't easy.'

'Why? What's up?'

She started chatting a bit about her problems with her boyfriend Dean, then she asked how I was.

'Well, actually, I'm pregnant.'

I heard her gasp then she made a little squeaking sound. 'Lisa Hoodless! I didn't even know you had a boyfriend!'

'His name's Tony. The baby's due in June.'

'Lisa, why don't you come up to my place this evening? We've got so much to catch up with. Please come.'

I still thought there was a chance I was being set up, that I would arrive there to find a gang of girls waiting to bully me, but something in Charlene's voice sounded sincere so I decided to take a chance.

Later that day, I walked up the hill and knocked on the door of her dad's house. She opened it and stepped outside and put her arms round me for a big hug. She didn't let go of me for ages and it was an amazing feeling. Any misgivings I might have had disappeared as soon as I saw her. It was as though the last six years had never happened.

We sat and we talked all evening – about our friends who had died in the car crash, about our boyfriends, about our families, about my baby, and we also talked, for the very first time, about the three days when we were held prisoner by Alan. It was like closing the circle; as though a piece of me had been incomplete for six years and now it was joined up again.

'Friends for life this time?' Charlene grinned at me before I left.

'Definitely,' I said, and meant it.

23

Charlene

On Friday 18 November 2005, Dean and I were out with my friend Dan, whom I'd known since primary school; he was the one who'd shown me round on my first day at Christchurch Primary and he'd become a close friend. There was also a girl called DJ who was in my year at school, and another girl called Kelly. We were in a graveyard that we called Churchie with about twenty other people and most of them were drinking. Earlier in the day, several of them had been at the funeral of a girl called Sherena who had fallen into a coma and died after someone spiked her drink with drugs. I had hardly known her, but other people there were really upset and they were getting blind drunk. I was the only sober one.

It started raining and it was getting very late, so I asked Dean to walk me home and we set off down the hill. After we left, Dan, DJ and Kelly met up with two other guys called Barry and Lee, who were in a stolen car. Apparently, they offered them a lift and for some reason I can't understand, Dan got into that car. He'd always been a really good boy, never in trouble with the police, while Barry was Dean's best friend and he was a naughty boy.

Although he was only fifteen, Barry was in and out of prison and known for stealing cars, so I was surprised that Dan would have taken a lift from him. But it was raining and he was a bit drunk, so maybe that was why.

A police car spotted the stolen car and gave chase. Instead of pulling over, Barry drove out to the Battle Road at top speed, where he skidded, lost control of the car, hit a lamppost and flipped over. None of them were wearing seatbelts and they all died instantly.

I got a phone call from a friend the next morning and Dean got one at the same time, and our first instinct was to go up to the crash site. I don't know why; I suppose I was in shock and I just wanted to understand what had happened because it didn't seem real. The car had been towed away but we saw the spot where the lamppost was bent over and a wall was smashed in. There were lots of journalists there with cameras and tape recorders and I gave an interview to one of them explaining that I had been with three of the dead people just before they got into the car.

It was hard to accept that I'd never see Dan again, never hear his voice on the phone saying 'Hi, Char, what's up?' It didn't seem right that people our age could die before they'd even done anything with their lives.

When I got back home, I was shell-shocked. I called a few friends to tell them what had happened but all the time there was something nagging at the back of my mind; something I had to put right. I got a really strong urge to ring Lisa and bring all the stupidity of the last few years to an end. I was sixteen years old, nearly seventeen, and I could look back and realise that she hadn't actually done anything wrong. I'd put her through hell for no reason when I was the one person who should have been there for her. I'd always protected her before that. I'd got into Alan's car that day to protect her. How could I have been so horrible to her afterwards?

I was so nervous when I picked up the phone that my hands were shaking and my chest felt tight. Did she still live with her dad? I didn't even know if I had the correct number. Would she speak to me if she were there? She would be well within her rights to hang up as soon as she heard my voice.

Her dad answered the phone and sounded perfectly friendly when I said who it was. 'Oh hello, Charlene. I'll just go and get her for you.'

Then Lisa came on the phone and I could tell she was wary of speaking to me but I just apologised right at the beginning of the call. Tears were rolling down my cheeks as I spoke. She agreed to come up and see me that evening, and we ordered takeaway chicken tikka masala and sat and talked about absolutely everything.

I told her about how I'd been annoyed when she got friendly with other people and I felt she wasn't being my best friend any more. She said she'd felt the same way but didn't know what else to do when everyone started crowding round us like that.

I told her how cross I was that she had stopped counselling before me, and it made me feel that she was getting over it and moving on, leaving me behind. She said she was really surprised I'd had to carry on with counselling but that it was down to the fact that our dads had different opinions about how useful it was.

She told me how depressed the bullying had made her, and all I could do was keep on apologising. I'd never thought before about what it must have been like to be on the receiving end of all that abuse. She said she felt worthless and stupid, as if she deserved it all. Every time she entered a room she had butterflies in her stomach wondering who was there and whether they were going to bully her. All those times when I had been egging people on to victimise Lisa I had never once stopped to think about what it must have felt like to be her, and I was horribly ashamed. I didn't deserve to be forgiven, but Lisa said it was fine, it was all ancient history now; she was just happy we could be friends again.

Then we talked about the abduction: about why I got into the car with her instead of running for help; about why Alan had targeted me most in the beginning; about the night on the cliff; about why we didn't run away when we were left outside the fish and chip shop; about Lisa walking in while he was trying to have sex with me at his parents'; about what had happened to us in the police station afterwards; about our experiences of counselling, and everything that happened in the aftermath. She mentioned things that I didn't remember and I reminded her of bits she'd forgotten. We found it fascinating, adding our memories together and filling in the gaps. It was therapeutic, in a way that counselling had never been, because we were old enough to understand more by then and to put it into context.

That night, we became friends as grown-ups rather than friends as children. Loads of friendships never make that transition anyway, but the differences between us didn't matter any more. We liked different music and different kinds of clothes. She liked going out clubbing whereas I would rather stay at home watching TV. But the things we had in common were so much bigger and more important than any differences that I knew for sure we would be friends for life now.

The friendship deepened even further in June 2006 when her little son Kyle was born and I became an honorary auntie. I adored him from the word go and was always happy to get down on my hands and knees and play with him. I'd always loved kids and when I left school, I went to college to do a child development course and then worked at a primary school and in an after-school club for four- to eleven-year-olds.

But before that, in May 2006 we got a huge shock when we heard that Alan Hopkinson had applied for parole. Dad only heard about it when he got a phone call from a reporter at the *Hastings & St Leonards Observer* looking for a comment from him. By the time we found out, the hearing was over and his application had been turned down, but it still came as a terrible surprise to think that it was even a remote possibility. Lisa, Dad and I talked about it and Dad made an official complaint to the police that we hadn't been informed in advance, as we should have been.

It started us worrying about it, though, and when a journalist from the *News of the World* got in touch with me just after my eighteenth birthday asking if I would like to tell my story, I decided to do it. Lisa said she would as well. We reckoned that by putting the details out there in the public domain, and letting the world know exactly what Alan Hopkinson had done to us, we would make it less likely that he would ever be allowed out to walk the streets again.

After we did the *News of the World* article, a TV company got in touch asking if they could make a *Cutting Edge* documentary for the BBC, and again we agreed, for the same reasons. However, there were some shocks in store as we found out more about the story than we had been told back in 1999.

We learned that Alan Hopkinson had been a bank manager, of all things. He'd been married and had a child, but in 1991 he was sent to jail for the attempted kidnapping of a seventeen-year-old French girl and the actual kidnapping of an eleven-year-old British girl. These were the ones he'd told us about when we were in the flat. He got out of jail in 1995 and that's when he moved to Eastbourne. A couple of years later he became friendly with two young girls there and he persuaded their mother to trust him by saying he had a kid of his own at home, so she let the girls come up to play with his computer. But it turns out he was doing a lot more than playing computer games with them when they came up to that flat – the same one where we had been held prisoner. They finally complained to their mother, who went to the police, and it was because of their complaint that the police visited Alan on that Friday morning back in 1999 when we were rescued. Otherwise we might never have been found. It was terrifying to think that our lives had hung on that chance visit. Our survival simply came down to lucky timing. I'm sure in myself that Alan would eventually have gathered up the courage to kill us. It was what he was working up to, I'm certain of it.

We learnt that when the police searched Alan's flat, they found a manuscript he had written about the rape of a thirteen-year-old girl, which seemed to be some kind of fantasy story he had made up. They found the maps with schools marked on them that we had seen in his office. They found all kinds of diary entries about someone called 'Arthur' and his paedophile adventures. And there were loads of books and newspaper cuttings about paedophilia and pictures of young children torn out of mail-order catalogues. It was sickening to realise just how dangerous and perverted he really was.

But the thing that was most shocking for me was the realisation that the night he took us up on the cliff top, we were actually at Beachy Head, a well-known suicide spot where the cliff is 530 feet above sea level, meaning that no one survives a jump or a fall from it. The *Cutting Edge* TV crew took us back there to do some filming and I felt very shaky as I looked around trying to work out where he had parked the car, and where he had almost pushed me over the edge. My legs gave out at one point and I had to sit down on the grass, breathing hard.

Apparently Alan Hopkinson had told the police that he planned to let us go and then jump off Beachy Head himself. He never admitted that he planned to kill us, but

I am certain in my own mind that I was close to death on the cliff top that evening, and that Lisa and I were in increasing danger with every hour we spent with him.

We also went back and filmed outside the flat where we'd been held, above a Tesco in Eastbourne. There is CCTV footage of Alan in there on the Thursday, buying the pizza and chips he fed us for our dinner, while other shoppers had no idea we were being held captive just three floors above.

I'm glad we made the documentary and got our story out there, to let people know what actually happened. There's nothing I'm ashamed of. Lisa and I had a narrow escape and we were very lucky to come out alive and relatively unscathed. It may sound like a crazy thing to say but I am actually glad I was abducted because it's part of what made me the person I am today.

I'm not totally unaffected by it, of course. I still don't like going out on my own at night and maybe I never will.

In the spring of 2008, my life took a very happy new turn. Since I was fifteen years old, I had been friendly with a boy called William and he'd been a good mate to me right through the whole period I was with Dean. He'd warned me not to get involved with him, but of course I didn't listen. When I broke up with Dean the first time, I went and stayed in William's flat, as a friend, and he looked after me, bringing me tea in bed in the morning and renting DVDs for us to watch, but he was upset when I went back to Dean again and we didn't speak for a while.

Gradually I realised that I felt jealous whenever I saw

William with another girl, but I was in denial and told myself that was just because I didn't want to share his friendship with anyone. My dad had liked him from the start and kept dropping hints that maybe I should go out with him, but I was a bit slow on the uptake.

When I broke up with Dean the final time, I texted William to say: 'I'm sorry. We need to talk.'

I didn't expect to hear back because he had been very annoyed with me, but I got a text by return and we met after college that day. Something had changed; when I looked at him, I somehow saw him with fresh eyes. I realised how handsome he was, and thought about how good he had always been to me. I felt as if my eyes had suddenly been opened and here, all along, the right man had been waiting for me. To my delight, William seemed to feel the same about me. Very soon, we had our first kiss. Then we started going out and before long, we were really and truly in love.

We've been together for over a year now and are expecting a baby in a few months' time. It feels as though William was the part that was missing, the healthy relationship I needed to make me enjoy life. I look forward to having our baby and making our own little two-parent family. One thing's for sure: our child will have a completely different upbringing from the one I did.

24

Lisa

Tony and I stayed together until Kyle was two years old but ultimately we didn't have enough in common and didn't love each other enough to make it work. By the time we broke up, I was relieved rather than sad, and now I can focus all my attention on my perfect little boy.

Motherhood was a complete revelation to me. I thought I'd known beforehand what it meant to love someone but I'd never experienced anything like the complete, overwhelming sensation I get when I look at Kyle. Just the tiniest things he does – like saying 'barjeypooh' instead of 'barbecue' or doing his Mr Tumble – give me butterflies in my stomach. The love is completely different from anything else in the world.

I was over the moon when Charlene got together with William and then announced she was pregnant. He's a gentle, kind guy and I get on well with him, which is lucky since I spend so much time with Char. She'll be a lovely mother and I know Kyle will be thrilled to have a little baby to play with. I hope they'll be good friends as they grow up.

I've got my own flat just down the road from

Charlene's, and I keep it obsessively clean and tidy just as I used to do with my bedroom at home. My sister Christine comes to stay sometimes but she knows she can't make a mess on my home turf. The only one who's allowed to leave things scattered around is Kyle, whose toys seem to get everywhere.

I'm up at Charlene's house every day at some point. We've both got other close friends as well but there's a depth to our friendship that you don't find more than once or twice in a lifetime. When you've been in a traumatic, life-threatening situation with another person, there are ties that link you for ever whether you like it or not. It would be the same if we'd been shipwrecked on a desert island or held hostage by terrorists. Extreme situations can bring out the best or the worst in you, and because we were so young we didn't always make the right decisions – but we made them together, as a team.

My little sister Georgie still lives at home with Dad and he's fiercely protective of her. She doesn't have half the freedom I used to have. I think he would like to keep her under lock and key if he could. I don't ever want to be like that with Kyle. When he's old enough, I'll have to let him go out with his friends but I'll be strict about knowing where he is and what time he has to be home. It would be impossible to protect him from all the sick people in the world, like Alan, without ruining his life in the process.

The three people who were most affected by our abduction were my mum, my dad and Charlene's dad. I know it will haunt them as long as they live and they'll never actually get over it. My mum and dad still won't talk about it. One day I was reading a book by Sabine Dardenne, a Belgian girl who was abducted and held captive by a paedophile for eighty days. She was kept in a horrid little cellar and as I was reading, I just felt so grateful that things were so much easier for Charlene and me. Mum couldn't understand why I was reading the book, though. She wouldn't touch it herself. She still gets panicky about how I'm going to get home when I've been out somewhere at night, or if she calls my mobile and I don't answer.

But the truth is that Charlene and I are fine. We're not alcoholics or drug addicts, as some people seem to expect us to be. We're young mothers who look forward to watching our children growing up and starting our careers, and I hope that we will always live near each other.

After a horrific, shocking event happens to you, you have a decision to make. You can decide to let it affect you or you can decide to put it behind you and move on. Charlene and I have both moved on. We will be best friends for life – not because we were abducted together but because we love one another.

Acknowledgements

We'd both like to thank Paulette Hearn for believing in us, and Gill for writing such a great book. It's come out exactly the way we wanted it.

Our individual thanks are as follows:

Charlene

Thank you to my dad, Keith, for giving me the best life I could ever ask for. Thanks to Lisa and all my friends for being there. And special thanks to William and Rubie-rae for giving me my happy ending.

Lisa

Thank you to all my friends and family, especially Sammi and Char. And huge thanks to Kyle for completing my life.